A Cameraman Abroad

A Cameraman Abroad

from Panorama to paranoia

n a t c r o s b y

The Larks Press

Published by the
Larks Press
Ordnance Farmhouse
Guist Bottom, Dereham
Norfolk NR20 5PF
01328 829207

Larks.Press@btinternet.com

Printed by the Lanceni Press
Garrood Drive, Fakenham, Norfolk

September 2002

Acknowledgements

A big thank you to my publisher Susan Yaxley of Larks Press for her encouragement.
Thanks to Grahame Whatling and Ron MacMorran for the picture on page 30, and to Stephen Denby for his shot of Vince and me on page 104.
Thank you to the many friends and colleagues, assistant cameramen, sound recordists, make-up girls, grips, lighting gaffers, best boys, prop men, laboratory representatives, assistant directors, editors, *Radio Times* and other photographers, who, over many years have supplied me with most of the production stills in this book. I apologize to them for having no record of their individual contributions.

N.C.

British Library Cataloguing-in-Publication Data
A catalogue record for this book is available from the British Library

ISBN 1 904006 06 X

Preface

I was having dinner with two friends in the village. We were swapping travel stories and, lubricated by the wine, were finding our experiences ridiculously funny. Suddenly Lesley said, 'You should write a book!'

'Oh no, not another cameraman's memoirs. There have been quite enough of those.'

However, when I arrived home later that evening, I thought about what she had said. Everyone has a book in them, so the saying goes. I had always enjoyed writing. At school I was quite often called upon to read my essay or story to the rest of the class. Being a show-off I enjoyed the experience.

During my thirty-one years with the BBC I had kept practically all my diaries. They contained such intriguing details as '£1 to man for loan of his ladder' and very little else. But I found that these sparse entries jogged my memory and details came flooding back.

What did I have to lose? Even though it was by then 1 a.m. I pounded away at my computer keyboard and continued to do so for the next two years.

When I thought I had almost completed the book, I began to realise that writing a book was one thing, getting a publisher to read it was something else. The rejection letters started flowing in. 'Sorry, not our kind of book, good luck!' 'Sorry we are being sent fifty manuscripts a week and cannot accept any more material, good luck.' 'Sorry, we only publish autobiographies of celebrities, good luck.'

It was cold comfort to learn that Charles Dickens's first work was rejected. He did at least get it serialised in a newspaper. Anyway, if Dickens had failed, what chance did my meagre efforts have?

Then one day I dared to make a phone call to a publisher instead of writing, something one is not encouraged to do. 'Bring it round' said an angelic voice at the other end. A short time later I handed it to her. 'Don't ring me, I'll ring you. I'll let you know what I think in about a month's time.'

A very long month later she did, and here it is.

I hope, dear reader, that you will enjoy this motley collection of triumphs and disasters, seasickness and homesickness, being fêted and arrested, meeting the great and the not so great, the famous and the infamous and those in-between.

N.C.

ABOUT THE AUTHOR

Nat Crosby was born 'on the fringes of East London' and began filming as an amateur, winning awards for writing and directing. After pestering the BBC with letters he achieved an interview and was asked if he wanted to be a 'trainee assistant cameraman' or a 'trainee assistant film editor. 'If he'd said trainee assistant floor-sweeper, I'd have been happy,' said Crosby. 'I randomly said "trainee assistant cameraman". It's strange how an instant decision can affect one's whole career.'

He spent thirty years with the BBC and won BAFTA awards for *Going Gently*, with Norman Wisdom, Fulton Mackay and Judi Dench, *An Englishman Abroad,* with Alan Bates and Coral Browne, and *The Insurance Man,* directed by Richard Eyre. He also won three Prix Italia prizes for *Mad Jack, The Spongers* and *Cruel Garden.* Other notable BBC productions filmed include *Ballroom of Romance, Silas Marner, East of Ipswich, Amy* (which he directed), and *Poppyland,* which began his love affair with Norfolk.

After leaving the BBC he shot *Nature of the Beast, Madame Sousatzka* (with Shirley MacLaine) *Monster Maker*, and *A Private Life*, which was shown at the London Film Festival. He now lives, by choice, in Norfolk and writes, produces, directs and photographs short drama productions.

The Piccadilly Line tube train had deposited me in an unfamiliar part of London. I left the traffic chaos of Ealing Broadway, made my way across the comparative calm of the green and suddenly there it was - the white gatehouse with two uniformed men guarding the entrance, the barrier down.

My mouth was dry and I felt a sudden surge of stage fright. I crossed the road and entered Ealing Studios, Ealing, famous for an era of outstanding British films such as *Passport to Pimlico, The Cruel Sea, The Lavender Hill Mob,* and now acquired by BBC Television to house their film department.

It was the summer of 1956 and my first day as a trainee assistant film cameraman. After many years as an amateur film-maker, and writing frequent letters asking for a job with the BBC, *any* job connected with television, to my amazement they finally said yes. Anything I suspect, to stem the flow of my entreaties. The conditions were that I was on probation and that I would have to learn to drive. I was 26 at the time and they said I was a little old to become a trainee but they would see how it went.

I was apprehensive. My previous job with A. B. Dalziell, ship's chandlers, seemed reassuringly undemanding. I was not certain if I would be able to absorb all this new technology *and* learn to drive. I knew I was not the brightest of people and that it often took a long time for things to sink in. As an amateur film-maker, I wrote, directed, photographed, edited (and sometimes appeared in) the little dramas I enjoyed making. But this was different. I would be the dogsbody, taking orders, being efficient and ordered, three things I didn't consider to be my best qualities.

For the first few days I was to standby in the camera room, where I would meet assistant cameramen and maybe even a real live cameraman. To get there meant walking past the front office, the canteen, the generator building, the Lot, a large square lined with the façades of houses and shops that I recognised from many Ealing films, then past cutting rooms, two big sound stages with their vast motorised doors, dubbing theatres and a labyrinth of iron staircases, suspended walkways and corridors, all the turmoil and excitement of a film studio. Three burley actors dressed as Mogul warriors were making their way to the canteen. Snatches of overheard conversation seemed strangely at odds with their appearance.

'...So I told him if he wants me to do *that* I should be paid extra!'

The camera room was a narrow shabby room with full-length metal lockers lining the walls and two or three padded chairs with their stuffing escaping. Assistants, perhaps to amuse their cameramen, had stuck all kinds of souvenirs on their masters' locker doors: photos, beer-mats, posters of foreign locations, nightclub flyers and cartoons that referred to private jokes.

The room was empty. Everyone appeared to be away on location. By the third day I was beginning to wonder if I would ever see anyone when a tall handsome man entered. This was, as I subsequently found out, Peter Hamilton, a very distinguished cameraman. I leapt out of my chair in deference to this Greek god. In the manner of the great and compassionate, he said 'Oh please don't get up.' It was too late; I was already up, bursting with questions. But my shyness got the better of me and I remained silent. After a minute or so he got bored with my company and left the room.

The next few months were blurred by their speed. As there was then no formal training school, I was assigned to various cameramen and their assistants. They showed me how to set up the bulky 35 mm film camera and equipment, load film magazines, fill in 'dope' sheets and after the day's filming had been completed, take the 'rushes' to the laboratory at Finsbury Park where the negative would be processed and a print made. I was longing to get my hands on the camera, but that was not allowed, apart from cleaning it of course.

Meanwhile I had passed my driving test in an old bouncy Ford Popular I had acquired, and began almost to enjoy the several near misses I experienced every day as I battled my way along the ruthless North Circular road.

I lived with my parents on the fringes of East London. My elder brother and sister, both married, lived nearby. I had to decide whether to stick with home comforts or find a bed-sit in Ealing thus avoiding a three-hour journey to and from the studios. I chose the former. I was often away on location so I would not be doing that journey every day; anyway I was enjoying my new-found driving skills. My father, a passionate amateur violinist, was a kind, patient and unassuming man who had spent the First World War in the Royal Army Medical Corps. If anyone felt unwell he was always ready with a remedy to make him or her feel better. As a child I remember his colourful bedtime stories. They were full of goblins and witches, a tale of a discontented fisherman's wife who finally wanted the moon, a ploughman who tilled the fields with his employer's horses and publicly proclaimed that they belonged to him. 'Gee up my five horses.'

He was very fond of the theatre, especially the music hall of his youth, and as a child I was taken to the pantomime at the local theatre, the Ilford Hippodrome. After a long climb up stone steps we were finally seated in the 'gods.' Then the pit orchestra, under the baton of Sidney Kaplin, would strike up a rousing overture, the curtain would suddenly glow with light and my heart would beat faster with anticipation. My father would build me model theatres, something in which I am still interested to this day. My mother, who made most of the household decisions, loved the cinema. There was a huge book entitled the *Picturegoer's Annual*, full of pictures of the stars and the studios with names like Culver City and MGM studios. Particularly impressive was a picture of an avenue of orange trees growing on Hollywood Boulevard. My mother knew who was married to whom, and all the other gossip dispensed by the studio's publicity department. Funds permitting I was taken at least once a week to afternoon shows at the local Regent Cinema. In between the films, there was a stage show with 'turns' and in the interval girls wearing black dresses and stockings, white aprons and white caps, served tea on trays. This was pleasure for the eye only, for to partake of the tea and little coloured cakes would have been well beyond our budget. It was the era of Greta Garbo, Fred Astaire and Ginger Rogers, Douglas Fairbanks and Tyrone Power, Bette Davies and Talulah Bankhead, Laurel and Hardy, George Formby and Gracie Fields.

We always seemed to be well fed in spite of my mother having to manage on the very low income that my father received. He was a tailor and made waistcoats on piecework in a Whitechapel sweatshop, although sweating was not an option in the middle of winter when one tiny two-bar electric heater was used to heat the freezing workshop. She was a good cook and we all looked forward to the large Sunday boiler chicken, plucked of its feathers in the morning, and turned into memorable meals for the next two or three days. On one occasion my father's weekly wage was seven shillings and sixpence. Rather than bring this paltry sum home he bought a bottle of Wincarnis Tonic wine with the money and handed this to my mother in lieu of her housekeeping. I remember being impressed by this hopeless extravagance, which made her smile in spite of her disappointment. They were good people and I dearly loved them.

After I had been to see a Fred and Ginger film, stunned by the huge sets, the lighting and the camera moves, I would build a miniature camera crane out of Meccano and make scenery out of cardboard tubes in my bedroom. I read everything in the public library that I could find about film-making, particularly accounts of the Great Russian directors of early cinema. Pudovkin's *Film Technique,* was a book that I read over and over again. I was fascinated by early experiments with film editing. They shot a close-up of an actor quite expressionless. They then cut this strip of film into 10-second lengths and inter-cut it with shots of a bowl of food, a lion roaring and a corpse. This was shown to an audience who were asked for their reactions. What a wonderful actor, came the response. How hungry he looked when he saw the bowl of food, how frightened when he faced the lion and how sad when he saw the corpse.

My education was interrupted by the Blitz on London by German warplanes in 1941. I was eleven and the grammar school I was to attend after just scraping by my eleven plus, was several miles away. This was at the height of intensive bombing raids on London. Bombs and landmines had destroyed two nearby houses in our street. We had abandoned the cold, damp, corrugated iron shelter half buried in the garden, and spent night after night during air raids, huddled under the stairs while my dad did his watch as a member the Home Guard. The space under the stairs was considered to be the safest part of the house if a bomb were to hit it. Mobile anti-aircraft guns made a tremendous racket in the streets outside as they moved around the area shooting at enemy aircraft.

In view of all this turmoil my parents considered it too dangerous for me to travel to the new school so I stayed at the local school and left as everyone else did, at fifteen. I took a drama course at the nearby Southeast Essex Technical College. I thought that I could become an actor or at least something to do with the theatre or films.

However the reality was somewhat different. My first job was in Austin Friars in the heart of the City of London with Messrs Foster & Braithwaite, stockbrokers. The mysterious world of high finance was partly revealed to me and one of my tasks was to deliver stock transfers every morning to various little top-floor offices all over the city and return in the afternoon to collect the cheques. I never really understood what it was all about and knew that this was not how I wanted to spend the rest of my life. Part of my lunchtime would be spent walking to Cheapside where I would press my nose against the window of Wallace Heaton's photographic shop. I wanted to make sure that the little second-hand cine camera, an Agfa Movex 8 that I had been keeping my eye on, was still unsold. It was £12 and after several months I had saved enough to buy it. At last I could make my own movies but I found that it wasn't *that* easy to make a Fred and Ginger film! So I concentrated on simpler subjects like my mother hanging out the washing and my father playing his violin. My sister, brother, sister-in-law brother-in-law and nephew were roped in as reluctant extras in the cheesy little dramas I started concocting.

At eighteen I was conscripted to do my National Service. I chose the Royal Signals as I had heard that there was an army projection unit going round to various camps showing films. It was only later that I found out that civilians ran this. After basic training at Catterick camp I took up my role as a radio teleprinter operator. I was posted to Singapore, my first trip abroad. We spent a magical month on the troopship *Orduna* with her permanent list to starboard, sailing through the lumpy Bay of Biscay, the glassy Mediterranean, the Suez Canal, the Red Sea and the Indian Ocean. I wrote long letters home, trying to describe it all, and took many photos with my old Ensign Selfix camera. I had left my movie camera behind since it was quite difficult to get film for it.

Singapore was a riot of colour and heat and since radio conditions were better at night, that was when our shift started, sending and receiving coded teleprinter messages to and from the War Office in London and the Australian Army in Melbourne. On one quiet evening I was nodding off when the door to the wireless room opened and the C.O. entered with a group of parliamentary VIPs on a Far Eastern tour. They surrounded my workstation. 'This man is in direct radio contact with the Australian Army in Melbourne,' the C.O. said proudly. The group was impressed. 'Call them up Crosby,' he ordered. We were working in duplex, which meant that any message I sent to Melbourne would not be printed on my teleprinter. We were supposed to stick to strict procedures when communicating, but usually it became a two-way conversation about the weather and other matters of world importance. I hammered out on my keyboard that I was surrounded by VIPs and to stick to correct procedures. There was a pause and then my machine started to print. The man in Australia seemed to be typing with one finger. Every one leaned forward to read the message from the Australian army, which read, 'You woke me up you Pommy bastard.'

During the day my colleague, Frank Crumbleholme and I would explore the exotic scenes in the town. The waterfront with its Chinese junks, the roof of the Cathay building where there was a fantastic view of the island and the crowded narrow streets bustling with street stalls amid a jungle of vertical signs in Malay and Chinese. Frank came from Ormskirk near Liverpool; we had made friends at Catterick before travelling together to Singapore. After National Service and a brief correspondence, we lost touch and I have often since tried to get in contact with him. I recently wrote to every Crumbleholme I could find on the Internet (there aren't that many) but without success. While in Singapore I joined an army drama group and we toured the army camps with a production of *The Ghost Train.* One of my fellow actors was Jeffrey Dench, Dame Judi's brother.

On my return to England, back to being a civilian, I spent three months in the massive electronics factory Plessey, and took evening classes in radio and electronics hoping that this would enable me to get work in Television. But my heart was not in becoming an engineer but in making movies. I returned to the City, this time to a ship's stores company in Bevis Marks where I attended to the customs formalities involved in shipping duty-free tobacco and spirits. My spare time was occupied with making amateur films and I received the 'Ten Best Amateur Films of 1953' award for one of them, a little thriller called *Headline.* I sent it to the BBC with yet another request for work.

Anna Neagle presents me with a certificate from Associated Rediffusion for my amateur film, *Beach Incident*. On the right, Lesley Mitchell

A Question

'What job would you like to do in the film department?' Offered the man from personnel. I was sitting in an office at Broadcasting House, hardly able to believe that I had finally penetrated its Portland Place portals.

'A director,' I said modestly.

'Yes yes, everyone wants to be a director. *I* want to be a director,' he snapped. 'I can put you down as a trainee assistant film cameraman or a trainee assistant film editor.'

I think if he had said trainee assistant floor sweeper I would have accepted. It seemed that my recurring dream of becoming a professional was about to become a reality. I often wonder what my life would have been like if I had taken the film editor option. Less stress perhaps, a more socially ordered life maybe, but not the excitement of whirling round the world at high speed, capturing images of the lives of people from many different cultures.

At Ealing

I was assigned to Charles de Jaeger and his assistant John Ray. Charles de Jaeger, a cameraman with a Viennese background, had achieved some notoriety by having the idea of a 'spaghetti harvest' April fool's joke. He had had the idea for some time and managed to persuade producer Richard Cawston to use it on the air. On Monday 1st April 1957, in the *Panorama* programme, noted for its impartiality and relentless pursuit of truth, Richard Dimbleby solemnly described the 'particularly good spaghetti harvest in the Po Valley' accompanied by pictures that Charles had shot of spaghetti hanging from trees. Such was Richard's reputation for integrity that a large number of viewers and a few senior BBC officials, totally accepted that pasta grew on trees.

Far from the Po valley, De Jaeger and Ray were shooting a three-week documentary in a mental hospital in Banstead, Surrey, and needed an extra pair of hands. The Hospital was a massive Victorian building and inside it resembled something between a Dickens novel and a Hammer horror film. My job was to unload the film magazines as they were exposed, put the film rolls in to cans, label them, record the shots in a dope sheet book and reload the magazines with fresh film. I had a large, black, light-proof changing bag with elasticised sleeves through which I could put my arms to manipulate the film magazine in the darkness of the bag. I sat in a busy corridor to do this and every so often John Ray would come along with the exposed magazines for me to unload, and to take away the freshly loaded ones. Since my arms were trapped in the bag he would take great delight in wrapping waste film round my head into a sort of celluloid turban and then go away. There were some pretty bad mental cases passing by but the inmates seemed to be relieved to see someone who was worse than they were! When we returned to Ealing at the end of a day's shoot, unloading the rushes was much simpler. There were dark rooms to use - rather than the awkward changing bag. One assistant, George Gibbons, for some inexplicable reason would always close his eyes when unloading the film. One evening with his eyes tightly closed as usual, he forgot to switch out the darkroom light and the day's rushes were ruined.

Later we were filming in a small square in London, and I was sent off to fetch a lens that was in the camera car, parked some way away. On the way back I took a wrong turning and with panic realised I was lost. When I eventually found the crew the cameraman shouted, 'Come on, come on, I am losing my light.' I had nightmares about that for a long time afterwards and cursed my poor sense of direction, which had almost resulted in Charles de Jaeger losing *his* light.

Eventually I finished my traineeship and became a full assistant. One day several of us were chatting in the camera room when an emotional assistant burst in. It was Ken Westbury and he was waving a piece of paper. 'I've got it. I've got the cameraman's job!' This was indeed exciting news. Up to that point, cameramen were appointed from outside the BBC, assistant cameramen being considered unsuitable candidates. Ken's promotion opened the way for all of us.

The first permanent cameraman I was to assist was Dougie Wolfe, a huge man with a hearty laugh. In his day he had been, among other things, an all-in wrestler before entering the film industry as a news cameraman. His wrestling skills were very useful when we were covering an event that was being attended by the rest of the jostling press photographers.

I spent two years with Dougie. A few months after I joined him he was to go to Australia, Malaya and India on a documentary called *The Inheritors* with Aidan Crawley as the reporter. I couldn't believe that I was to accompany him to these amazing places. Then came a bomb-shell. The front office had decided that I was too inexperienced to do such a trip. They reasoned that if Dougie became ill they needed someone who could take over. I knew, and Dougie knew, that I could do this. He used to let me operate the camera while he attended to the lighting. Great experience for me and he seemed pleased with my work. He dug his heels in and said he would not go on the trip without me. The office relented and I was to do the job after all.

There were five of us travelling: producer Tony de Lotbinière, reporter Aidan Crawley, Dougie Wolfe, sound man Dave Ziegler and myself. The journey started with

Early days at the BBC

a flight to Australia, and took three days in a Quantas Super Constellation, staying overnight in hotels en route. Very different from travel today.

I think I enjoyed Australia most of all. We filmed in Sydney, Canberra, Perth, Darwin, Adelaide and Brisbane. We took the long flight from Sydney to the small central Australian town of Alice Springs in a twin-engined DC3. The seating was very cramped and during the bumpy flight Aidan Crawley eventually had to move his long legs into the gangway to ease the pain. A blonde stewardess with glossy lips approached and slapped his legs. 'Move yer feet in,' she ordered, 'want me to go flat on my fice?'

We finally landed at the airstrip and off-loaded the gear and ourselves into two hired cars and headed for the Alice Springs Hotel, looking forward to a bath and a meal. The owner, a kind elderly little lady, greeted us at the hotel's reception desk. 'Good day, gentlemen, and welcome to our luxury hotel. I'll be delighted to show you to your suite,' she said graciously. We followed her with some anticipation. The suite turned out to be a large room with five beds. The hotel's dress code was strict. There was a sign in the bar that read, 'Gentlemen must wear singlets after 6 p.m.'

Alice Springs is in the centre of Australia's vast arid interior. We were there to film life on an outback cattle station, near the mystical Ayers Rock, and to do a piece on the School of the Air, a school conducted by two-way radio for the children living at too great a distance to attend.

After a month we had finished the Australian part of the film series and moved on to Malaya and then to India, a three-month trip in all. For me, the journey was a unique experience, but I don't think it was a good trip for Dougie. He and the director, Tony de Lotbinière didn't get on and hardly spoke to each other. The heat and the gruelling schedule made things worse. On non-filming evenings when the rest of us would go to a restaurant, he stayed in his room writing long letters to his wife. It can be a lonely life away on location in spite of being in exotic places, and the longer one is away the more the tensions build.

Back in England Dougie Wolfe was again a cheerful companion whose hearty laugh miraculously failed to unseat the cigarette constantly dangling from his lips. Sadly he was to die in his fifties, from lung cancer. My first cameraman, I shall never forget him.

Sophie Tucker

Older readers might remember Sophie Tucker, an American nightclub singer and film star somewhat in the mould of Mae West, who was famous for the spoken delivery of her risqué songs. She was appearing at the Café de Paris in London, and Dougie and I were to go along and shoot some film of her during a special performance for our camera. On the morning of the shoot I was called in to the film operation office. 'Doug's not well,' said the allocations manager. 'Can you do this one on your own? You can take a trainee as an assistant.' I of course said yes, and we set out for the Café de Paris with camera, sound and lights.

A cleaning lady wielded a vacuum cleaner and the interior of the nightclub with its blazing work-light revealing flaking paintwork and threadbare curtains had lost some of its night-time glamour. The two electricians and I set up the lights, the soundman his mikes, and we waited for Miss Tucker to appear.

A door at the back of the room opened. A minder and Miss Tucker's accompanist were helping in a frail old lady in her eighties. The room filled with her personality in a most remarkable way. This was star quality of a kind that I had not experienced before. I approached her shyly through the waves of magnetism, introduced myself and checked her lighting. Her face close-to showed the effects of a long life of travelling and performing, the endless venues in anonymous towns, faceless hotels, too many martinis, late suppers, railway stations and touring buses. I adjusted a light and softened it with a diffuser. 'Are you going to make me look beautiful honey?' she asked, in a voice that sounded like a hacksaw rubbing against the strings of a cello. I gave her a reassuring smile as if I had been doing this all my life. The lights were dimmed and the camera turned.

Her pianist struck up the opening bars of her signature tune and Sophie Tucker began her performance of 'Life begins at 40', no doubt for the many thousandth time. There was a remarkable transformation. The years dropped away from her, and her eyes sparkled. The voice was clear, the phrasing and timing perfect. Everyone in the room fell under her spell.

Losing focus

Although Dougie was my regular cameraman, if he were away on leave or for some other operational reason, I would be assigned to assist another film cameraman. On one of these occasions I was to assist the legendary A. A. Englander.

No one knew what the two initials meant but it was rumoured that one of them stood for Adolf. 'Tubby', as we were allowed to call him, although he was not in the least portly, was a fierce disciplinarian. His black moustache bristled with disapproval at the slightest perceived misdemeanour of his crew. As his assistant it was considered prudent to spend any spare time polishing Tubby's large aluminium equipment cases and trying to keep out of trouble. Most assistants were a little scared of his sharp tongue and threatening smile, including me. On this occasion we were to shoot a drama sequence on stage 3A at Ealing.

The script called for a slow tracking shot that started as a wide shot and finished as a big close-up of one of the actors. Rails were laid by the grip, the heavy dolly lifted on to them and the camera set up on the dolly. Tubby asked for a 100 mm lens. This was rather a long lens for this type of shot. As an assistant part of my job was to keep the subject in focus as the camera moved in. I had a focus control linked to the lens and did a series of measurements with a tape at various positions along the track. Marks were made at various points so that I could synchronize the lens focus settings. There were three problems for me. One, the camera movement was extremely slow so any focus errors would be clearly seen on the screen. Two, the wide aperture being used on the lens meant that there was an infinitesimal margin for focus error. Three, the four-inch lens had much less depth of field than a wider lens. This meant in practice that if I got it only slightly wrong, the actor's nose could be sharp instead of his eyes, and due to the slowness of the move it would be very obvious. After a brief rehearsal we did two takes, checked that the gate was free of 'hairs' (minute slivers of film that could appear in the aperture of the camera gate, thus ruining the take) and then moved on to the next scene.

I had a sleepless night punctured by fitful dreams of blurred actors inter-cut with terrifying close-ups of a bristling moustache.

The next morning I left home at the crack of dawn to see the rushes in a viewing theatre at Ealing. The North Circular road seemed even more threatening than usual, with an unprecedented number of moustached drivers cutting in and out of the heavy traffic. After several hold-ups I finally arrived at the studios in a somewhat emotional state.

The small rushes theatre contained about two dozen cinema seats. Camera crews who were working in the studio or nearby were expected to come along to see their previous day's work. In addition to Tubby and I and two other cameramen and their assistants, there was a film operation manager and his assistant, a laboratory representative, and two engineers, all eagle-eyed to spot technical errors. If any error were spotted it was usually marked by a sharp intake of breath from one of the technical mandarins. The effect of this sound on the unfortunate culprit be it cameraman or assistant, was more startling than a pistol shot.

We started by seeing another crew's rushes, and they seemed to go on interminably. Actually their quality was good and a certain amount of self-congratulation took place. Eventually our rushes came on to the small cinema screen and the first part was OK. Then the tracking shot appeared. On take one I lost focus for about half a second about a third of the way through. There were several sharp intakes of breath and I considered making a run for it but abandoned the idea as I was seated in the middle of a row. Then came take two. To my relief that was OK and the director who was also in attendance preferred the actor's performance in that take.

I polished Tubby's cases yet again.

A Vacancy

Outside the camera room was a notice board. As I approached a group of assistants were reading it. There was a vacancy for a cameraman and applications were invited both from within the BBC and from outside. Applicants had to appear before a board of some eight senior BBC staff and Heads of Department who would assess their suitability. The conference room where the boards were taking place was in the same block as the canteen. The five applicants to be seen that day, myself included, were nervously drinking coffee in the canteen, wearing our best suits in readiness for our entry into the lions' den. When it was my turn I rose from the table feeling far from confident. The main entrance to the conference room was outside the canteen opposite the generator building. It was also accessible from a door in the canteen and since I was in the canteen I chose that entrance. This proved to be a mistake. The opening door revealed a line of eight people sitting with their backs towards me facing the other entrance. I light-heartedly made the long journey round to the chair on the other side. No one appeared to find this remotely amusing and my heart sank. The interview is a blur but I remember the chairman saying 'Oh, you're using the other entrance this time,' as I left. Eddie Best told me afterwards that at the end of his interview he had risen with great dignity and walked straight into the broom cupboard. Another applicant George Gibbons said he was so nervous that to break the tension he offered every one of the board a cigarette. One by one they solemnly refused. He returned the pack to his pocket not daring to take one himself.

A week went by and there was still no news. Then on the 28th November, 1960, I learnt I had become a fully-fledged cameraman. Hallelujah!

Lowest Spot in the World

My first assignment in my new job was to shoot a story in the Middle East over Christmas, with reporter Trevor Philpot and Professor Allegro of Manchester University. The professor was studying the Dead Sea Scrolls that had been found by Bedouins in caves in a remote area near the Dead Sea, and was to return to Jordan to search for more scrolls. Our three-man crew was to be based in a hotel on the shores of the Dead Sea, and make sorties on foot into the desert where we were to meet the professor and stay under canvas with the expedition. In between we would be doing other stories, such as Christmas day in Bethlehem. This proved to be a bizarre day with recorded carols being blasted out of street loudspeakers including Bing Crosby's rendering of 'I'm dreaming of a White Christmas', and arguments among the various religious denominations over violations of praying times at the church of the Holy Sepulchre.

At the end of the day we found a restaurant and had a Christmas dinner of goat and chips and a bottle of the local wine Latroun, which we immediately renamed 'Latrine'.

But back to the Dead Sea. The taxi we had hired from Jerusalem passed through the biblical wilderness, an extraordinary moon-like landscape. The Dead Sea is 1,300 feet below sea level and as the taxi approached our ears popped as if we were landing in an aircraft. Then a sign appeared, 'Welcome to the lowest spot on earth'. Shortly after this we reached the Dead Sea Hotel. This was palatial, a

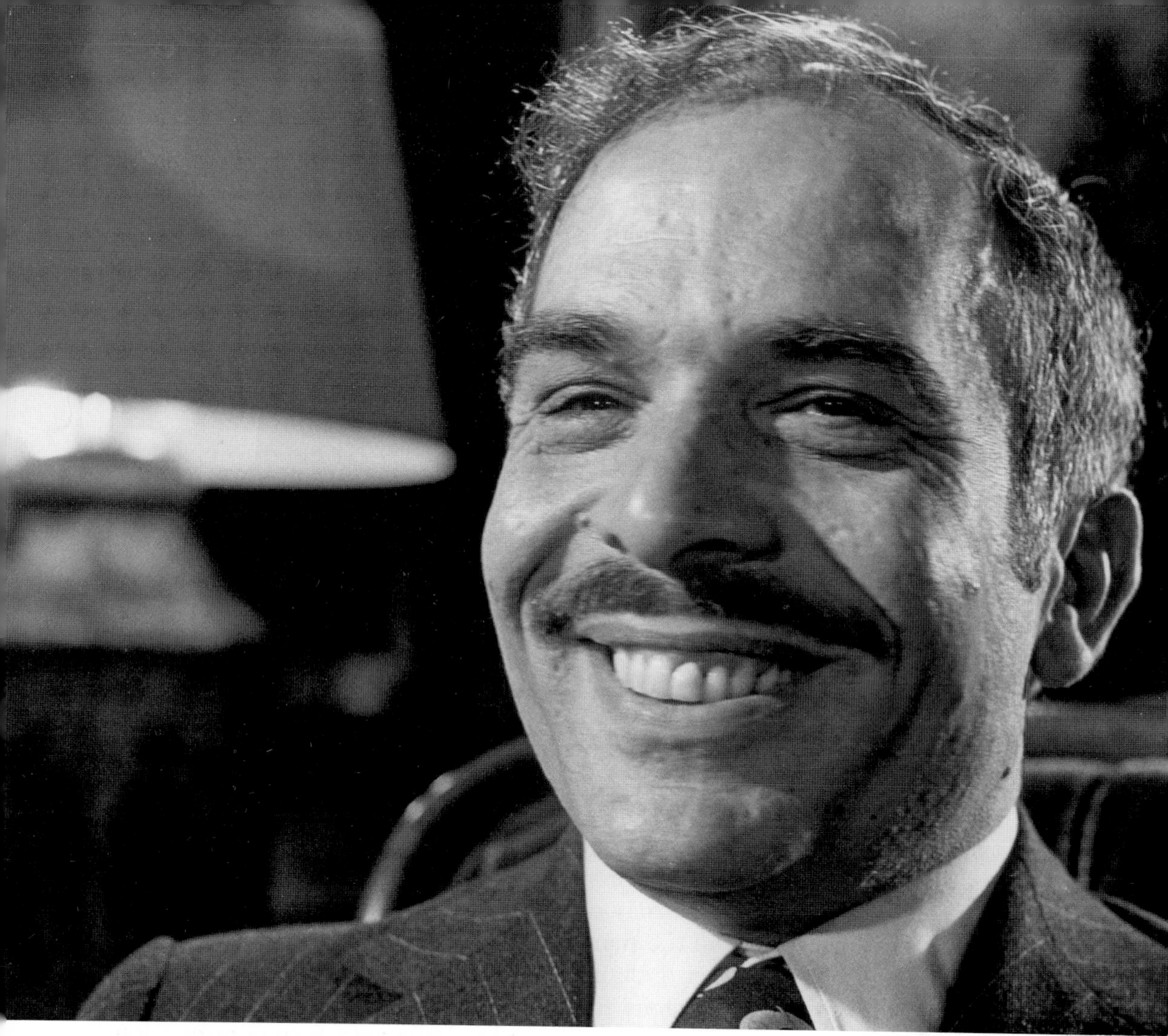

At Christmas King Hussein sent a supply of beer to the Dead Sea expedition

white elephant that had not been as successful as a tourist centre, as the Jordanian government had hoped. The staff numbered about thirty but there were only three guests, reporter Trevor Philpot, soundman Reg Crawley and myself. In spite of the opulence there were one or two amenities missing, like hot water. Since we were about to go into the desert the manager promised that the hot water system would be fixed by the time we returned in about five days. Having left as much of the baggage as we could at the hotel we set off in the taxi which was able to travel about four miles before the track became too rough. We continued on foot with the camera, film, tripod, lenses and sound equipment, a journey to the camp of about six miles. As it was winter the temperature was a perfect 72 degrees. The rocky terrain stretched ahead and the Dead Sea lay peacefully gleaming on our left. On the way we came across a goat herdsman who joined us to help carry the gear, cheerfully leaving his goats behind.

Eventually we arrived at the camp, tired and hungry and gratefully ate the plates of under-cooked freeze-dried Vesta's Paella that we were offered. A Jesuit priest handed me a glass of arak claiming it would keep the multitude of persistent flies away. I obediently drank the fiery aniseed spirit though I am not sure if it worked since it was difficult to judge how many flies there would have been without it. We were too exhausted to linger for long at the campfire gathering. We found our tents and collapsed.

It must have been about three in the morning when I left my tent to have a pee. There was a faint click. I looked round and a few yards away was an Arab with a rifle pointing at me. He was a Bedouin, one of several hired to guard us. Apparently other Bedouin tribes were jealous of our tribe's employment, and were liable to wreak their revenge, hence the armed guard. Fortunately he recognised me so I was able to climb back into my tent in one piece.

For the next few days we interviewed and followed members of the expedition as they searched more caves near the ancient village of Qumran. I came across the handle of a Roman jug that had presumably lain undisturbed for more than two thousand years. Several fragments of scrolls were found which would eventually be sent to the University in Jerusalem where studies were continuing.

After five days of filming in the desert we were about to return to the Dead Sea Hotel, and looked forward to a much-needed bath. This time we didn't have to walk. King Hussein had sent an army helicopter with a supply of beer for the expedition, and we hitched a ride back to the hotel.

Upon our arrival I sprinted up the staircase to my room, into the bathroom and turned on the tap. Cries of dismay could be heard from the other two rooms. The water was ice cold. I found the manager and pointed out that he had broken his promise. A few minutes later a chain of waiters appeared passing champagne buckets full of hot water up the stairs from the kitchens and emptying them into the three baths. The scene was reminiscent of a De Mille epic. It took quite a long time to fill each bath in this way, but it was worth the wait.

The Shadow of your Smile

Just through the studio gates at Ealing lay the front office. On the first floor the Head of Films and his team resided. On the ground floor stood the Film Allocations office. Requests for film crews from the various production departments were allocated from here. In charge of allocations was an affable Greek Cypriot called Reno Wideson. When he was giving us our assignments, he spoke slowly, wisely and justly, and a large smile was never far from his handsomely swarthy features. The smile was often a warning that a slightly unpleasant task was in the offing.

'How would you like to shoot a film on a nice sea voyage?' he asked me one day.

'Great, Reno,' I said. He smiled.

'It is a three-week trip on a Hull trawler.'

On another occasion as I entered the office his teeth sprang into action. 'Ah Nat,' he smiled, 'how would you like to do a nice documentary in the Middle East?' I nodded. 'It is over Christmas,' he grinned.

'Can I check?' I said. 'I had made other arrangements.'

The smile switched to full beam. 'It is either that or Sportsview.' This was the ultimate threat. Very few cameramen liked working on Sportsview.

Sporting Life

I did my Middle Eastern documentary and when I got back I was assigned to Sportsview anyway. It was a popular programme with viewers, but for cameraman it was all kick and rush with very little of the shot material reaching the screen. However, I took up my post with enthusiasm and prepared for my first job, which was to cover a football match.

Unlike today's multi-camera coverage, there was just one film cameraman (me) covering the match. I have to confess to not being a very avid football fan. As someone who knew little about the game, I was feeling slightly nervous, especially as, unlike using electronic cameras with their monitors, no one but me could see the pictures I was getting.

The match took place in Bradford. A scaffolding tower for the camera had been erected which was just about out of reach of the exuberant fans although that didn't prevent them from hurling humorous comments and the odd bottle at us when they became bored. I would like to have been able to report which teams were playing and what the final score was, but the memory of that afternoon is a blur. During the match my assistant unloaded and canned the rushes, discarding any of the 10-minute film rolls that didn't contain goals. There was no point in having these developed. When the game was over we drove to Bradford station and put the rushes on the train. They would be picked up at King's Cross station by the laboratories, developed overnight and a print sent to a film editor at Ealing. He would prepare the film to be transmitted in Sportsview that evening.

We were staying in a Bradford hotel since several other stories were being shot in the region. The next evening Les Kettley, part of the Sportsview production team, led the way to the lounge to watch the programme on the hotel's television set. I wouldn't say I was nervous but the butterflies in my stomach were doing Swan Lake. A waiter was serving a tray of Double Diamond to a group of commercial travellers and several people in the lounge were watching a programme on ITV. 'Does anyone mind if I switch to the BBC?' said Les in his impeccable Welsh accent. He took the ensuing silence to be affirmation and switched over. Up came the football match.

I didn't think my coverage was too bad. With my sense of drama I tended to concentrate on the disappointment of the goalkeeper when he let a goal in, rather than go with the other team's euphoria. Admittedly this was a different approach for Sportsview. Also my ball-anticipation could perhaps have been better and there were one or two situations where the ball went one way and my camera panned in the opposite direction.

The hotel lounge slowly emptied, and a silence fell on Les. He finally spoke. 'I think you'd better concentrate on boxing from now on, boyo,' he said.

The rest of my stint on Sportsview consisted of boxing stories and football and athletic training sessions, motor rallies, motor cycle scrambles and cycling events. I filmed Stanley Mathews entering the football ground for his first game with Stoke. I covered the 1962 Monte Carlo Rally, travelling in a participating Roots car which involved staying awake for four exciting days and nights. I did several stories with runner Adrian Metcalfe who was then studying at Oxford. He was always pleased to see me, saying that after being surrounded by so much rarefied academia it was refreshing to talk to an ignorant cameraman. I *think* he meant it as a compliment.

I enjoyed the excitement of filming ringside at boxing matches, in spite of getting spattered by blood, saliva, sweat and goodness knows what else. I filmed the Henry Cooper-Caldwell bout at Wembley. At the end of a match I would leap into the ring to capture the inevitable mayhem. That was usually the most exciting moment. There was a promising young British boxer at the time called Billy Walker, managed by his brother George. George Walker was to achieve a different kind of fame in the business world. In those early days George and Billy ran a garage in Plaistow and I filmed them serving petrol and servicing cars. Behind the pumps on the forecourt lay their house. Entering this was like stepping into another world. Designer décor, amphorae, antiques and boxing trophies greeted the eye, a contrast to the rather dingy world outside.

I did a lot of stories with soundman Fred Clark and he, Burney my assistant and I were away on location somewhere in the West country and were due to travel back to London that evening. We had had a rather good dinner at the hotel and none of us felt like travelling. We had a plan. Fred made a recording of the water streaming from the shower in his bathroom and we took his tape machine to a nearby phone box. Fred played the tape as I phoned Ronnie Spillane, the Sportsview organiser. 'Terrible weather here Ronnie,' I said. 'I don't think we're going to be able to make it back tonight.'

'I know, I can hear it, sounds like a monsoon,' Ronnie said sympathetically. 'It's strange, it's OK here. Look, you lads stay the night and come back tomorrow.'

Tonight in Ireland

In those days BBC TV used to shut down at 6 p.m. every evening and then reopen at 7 p.m. It was decided to fill this blank hour with a new magazine programme called Tonight. I was allocated to the programme to shoot film stories. Reporters such as Alan Whicker, Fyffe Robertson, MacDonald Hastings, Polly Elwys and

Filming a lobster fishing story with Alan Whicker and Mike Tuckner in Maine U.S.A.

Derek Hart, toured the country with a young production assistant and the camera crew, scanning the local papers for oddball stories that would make good material for the programme.

One particularly pleasant trip was to Southern Ireland. We did stories on Blarney Castle, leprechauns and a delightful matchmaker who was much in demand for introducing suitable couples in the sparsely-populated area around Killarney. Alan Whicker interviewed him in his inimitable style.

I have at this point to explain a 'cutaway'. It was usual to use just one film camera on these stories. Alan Whicker would be out of the picture alongside the camera asking the questions while the camera would be focussed on the person being interviewed, in this case Paddy the matchmaker. We would shoot considerably more material than could be used in the programme, so that the editor could use the most interesting bits and cut out the rest. However in order to avoid jumps in the interview, the cutaway was born. At the end of the interview, the interviewee would be thanked and released, the camera focussed on Alan, who would then repeat his questions and do a few understanding nods. The editor could then insert these into the shortened main interview to avoid awkward jumps or 'jumpcuts' as we called them.

After the interview I began shooting Alan's cutaways. He repeated all the questions and then did his 'noddies' convincingly to the empty air. It was after shooting several minutes of these that I noticed a man in the background of the picture, digging the garden. It was Paddy the matchmaker! It would have been too surreal to have Paddy in close up *and* in the background, so the puzzled Paddy was sent in to his house and we did all the cutaways again.

During our Irish tour we read in the local paper that many people were claiming to be related to the new president of the United States, John F. Kennedy. An advert was placed, inviting relatives to join us in the pub at New Ross. Sure enough the pub was packed with Kennedys. Over a hundred turned up, all claiming to be relatives of the President. There were poems, jokes and sparkling conversation, which soundman Don Martin and I did our best to capture on film. The party went on until 2 a.m. when the local policeman arrived and said the pub had to close. However he was gracious enough to accept a drink first while he told us that he was a Kennedy and he *knew* he was related!

Prime Ministers and Tigers

In April 1961 I was to work on a major documentary entitled 'Faces of Asia'. It was a nine-week shoot, travelling to Thailand, Burma, East Pakistan, India, West Pakistan and Afghanistan. The theme was a look at the countries surrounding China's borders, and how they were affected by their huge, and somewhat threatening neighbour. The director was Derek Holroyde and he was using local presenters in each country. His assistant was Stephanie Brown, the soundman Don Martin, and my assistant Ken Lowe, a Lancashire Lad. Ken, who had not travelled to such far-flung places before, was determined not to eat the local food. This was not too difficult since most of the hotels catered for European palates. Personally I like trying local delicacies and feel that the sooner one's stomach gets used to them the better. Ken however was adamant that he would only eat hotel food and when, during the day, the only alternative was a local café or food stall, he would stay in the car. Unfortunately he was the one to go down with dysentery and we had to leave him at the hotel for a few days under the care of the local doctor. Eventually, though not completely recovered, he was able to join us again.

In those days BBC travelling film units were considered something of a novelty and in each country we visited we were invariably invited to cocktail parties at the British Embassy. Ken was particularly successful at these social events. I saw him on one occasion surrounded by three girls from the embassy earnestly discussing his dysentery experiences. In turn they related theirs. It seemed that this subject was extremely popular on the cocktail circuit of the Far East. At one of these parties in Afghanistan I asked a member of the embassy staff what she did in her spare time. 'We put on musicals,' she said, 'we've just finished a run of *The Sound of Music*. I was surprised.

'How did that go down?'

'Oh it was a resounding success,' she said. 'The *whole* of Kabul came.'

'Didn't the audiences have a problems with the language?' I asked.

'Oh I don't mean the Afghans!' she said sharply.

We were to film five hundred Afghan schoolgirls singing their National Anthem. Ken held the clapperboard up to the camera as usual. This was used to ensure that the editor would later be able to keep the sound synchronised with the picture. 'One hundred take one,' he announced and clapped the board. The schoolgirls instantly burst in to song. This wouldn't have given the film editor room to 'get the scissors in' and Ken was having none of this. 'No. Not yet,' he cried. It took some effort to stop five hundred Afghan schoolgirls in full spate but he eventually succeeded. We tried again. 'One-hundred take two,' called Ken and clapped. It happened again. The girls surged into song. Ken yelled in his best Lancashire accent, 'No! Wait while we're ready!'

In Delhi we were planning an interview with the Prime Minister, Jawaharlal Nehru. The interview was to take place in the early evening at the Prime Minister's residence. I was there in the afternoon with two electricians from the local film studio to light the room where the interview was to occur. I was adjusting the film lights when a man dressed in white appeared at the doorway. 'What's going on here?' Mr Nehru demanded. 'We're getting ready for your interview, sir,' I replied. 'I see.' he said. 'You should be filming my tiger cubs, would you like to see them?' I nodded and he led the way into the garden. There were five tiger cubs playing on the lawn. These weren't the small cubs I was expecting but were sort of teenage tiger cubs, and they were surrounding me and playing with my shoelaces in a slightly alarming way. 'They are getting too big, I must send them to the London zoo,' the Prime Minister chuckled. His simple humility belied the importance of his office.

I was to photograph Pandit Nehru several times and to be present at his funeral on the banks of the Ganges. It was an extraordinary scene with his cremated body on a tower and the sons raking through the ashes and putting bones into urns. While filming this for Panorama, a sudden gust of wind covered me with ashes, a strange and moving experience.

'They are Spies'

August 1961. During a trip to the Berlin wall for Tonight, the East Germans arrested reporter Trevor Philpot and myself. I had been filming through the Brandenburg gate much to the annoyance of the East German guards. Then I accidentally took a step forward over the line and we were grabbed and frog-marched to a small room in the eastern sector. My film was confiscated and we were questioned about our motives and what we were attempting to illustrate. We

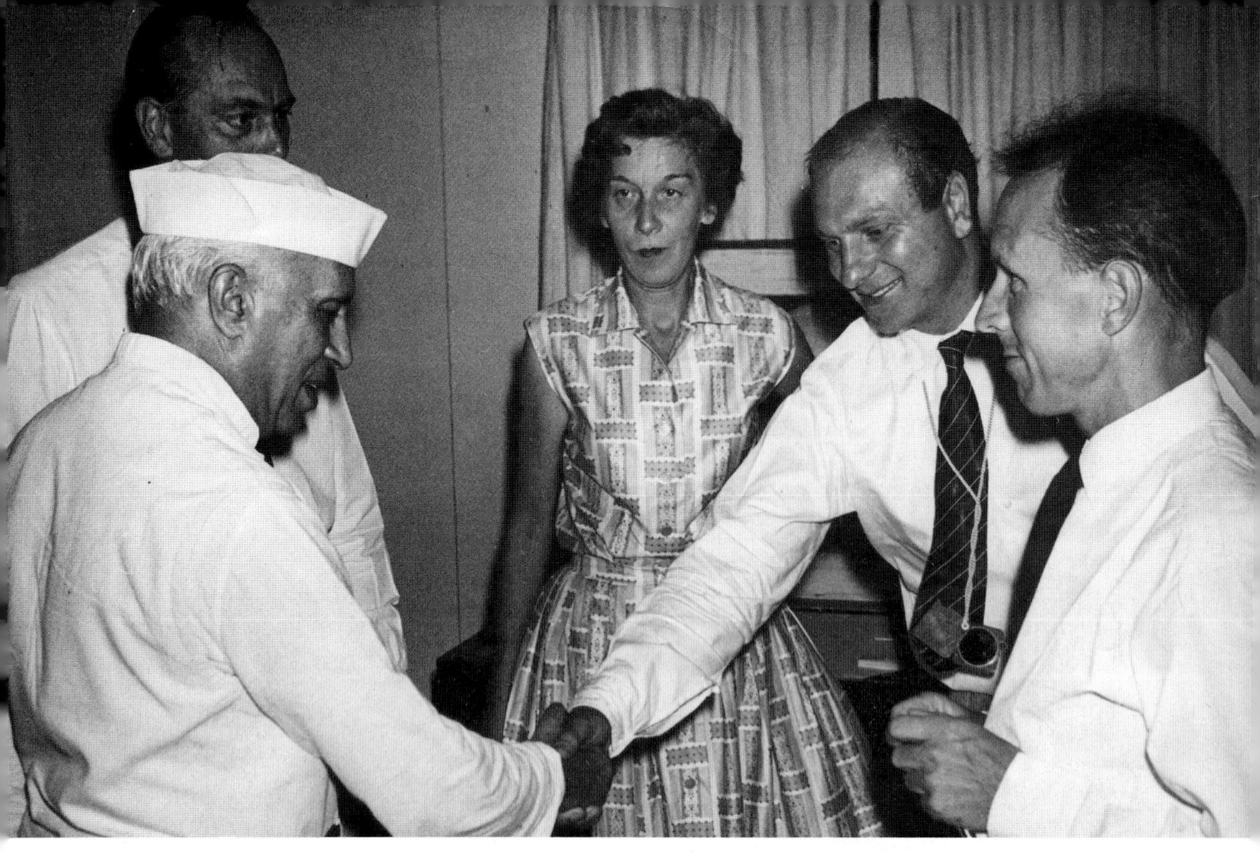

Meeting Prime Minister Nehru in Delhi, 1960
Left to right: Derek Holroyde, Prime Minister Nehru, P.A. Stephanie, Nat Crosby, Assistant Ken Lowe
Below: Shooting an interview with Prime Minister Nehru in Delhi

were left alone for long periods; presumably the room was bugged and they were hoping we would incriminate ourselves. We were there for about three hours before being released. The rest of the crew had alerted London and we became an item on the one o'clock news. Lesson to be learnt? Watch where you put your feet.

I was to be arrested again just over a year later while working for Panorama in Ghana. There had been an assassination attempt on the president, Dr Kwame Nkrumah. We arrived in Accra on 24th September, Robin Day, Grahame Whatling the soundman, and me.

Robin Day with the Panorama crew at the Equator

Because of the crisis, Ghana was under martial law and the atmosphere was tense. That morning Robin Day was to visit the ministry of defence to get permission to film, arrange interviews etc., while Grahame and I wandered around picking up any background pictures we could find. 'Wallpaper' as we called it, material that could be put on screen for Robin to speak over. We came across a parade ground with a battalion of soldiers drilling. It all seemed pretty innocent and I raised my Arriflex camera and began filming. After a minute or so there were shouts and army officers and a civilian in a bright flowered shirt surrounded us. He was furious. 'How dare you reveal our secrets?' the civilian shouted. His face was twisted with rage and I thought it would be better to address the senior officer who seemed much more reasonable.

'It's all right,' I said reassuringly, 'Mr Robin Day is at the Ministry of Defence and he has obtained permission to film.' If it were possible, the man in the flowered shirt became even angrier.

'I *am* the Minister of Defence, I know nothing about it. They are spies; hang them.'

Trying to defuse the situation I said, 'I haven't actually taken any pictures'.

'We saw you raise your camera,' retorted the Minister.

'I was checking the light,' I lied.

'I will see if you are lying. Arrest them.' We were bundled into a lorry under armed guard, and taken to an office at H.Q.

'Give me your film,' an officer said. I opened the side of the magazine, knowing that this would fog the film. I knew I hadn't taken anything worth saving. I took the roll out and gave it to him. 'We will have this developed,' he said. Fortunately his knowledge of photography seemed limited. An hour later they reported that the film was blank and we were released.

We were finishing our story a few days later when a cable arrived from Paul Fox editor of Panorama, authorising us to fly back first class, a rare event! The contrast of stepping from the searing heat and humidity into an air-conditioned Bristol Britannia and being greeted by two immaculate, smiling stewardesses was too much. Robin Day and I had a pillow fight in the empty first-class cabin. Robin was a very different person in the flesh from his image on screen as one of the new tough political interrogators. He was a jolly man with a schoolboy sense of humour. All the famous reporters I worked with were very much part of the team and our working relationships were democratic - one of the nice things about working for the BBC.

Mistaken Identity

Often when we arrived in a town, either at home or abroad, it was necessary to get some establishing material of the place, 'wallpaper' as I referred to it earlier. Grahame and I were doing just that in Lagos, Nigeria. I had taken about six shots of various buildings and streets, and was running out of ideas. It was very hot and a cold beer was beckoning, when a tall thin man came up to us. 'Come, I show you the Holy Ghost,' he said, in a deep, rich voice.

Grahame and I looked at each other. 'That's very kind of you,' I said, 'but we're rather busy just now.'

'No, no, no, no, you must come with me, I will show you the Holy Ghost,' he insisted. It was too hot to argue so after another feeble protest, we followed him. He led us to a modern building, into the lift and out at the top floor. We climbed a staircase and came out on to a flat roof. 'There you are,' he waved his arms proudly, 'the Holy Ghost'. Suddenly the penny dropped. He was actually saying he would show us *the whole of Lagos!*

Symphony

February 1963. I think that one of my most memorable journeys was by train to Prague, Warsaw, Moscow and St Petersburg (Leningrad as it was then) for the Music and Arts department. Producer John Drummond, my assistant John Else and I were covering four concerts being given by the BBC Symphony Orchestra under the batons of John Barbirolli and Pierre Boulez. The soloists were Jacqueline Dupré, John Ogden, and Janet Baker.

It was the middle of winter and everyone was aboard a special train from Paris to Prague where the first concert was to take place. It was a bit of a mad scramble for John Else and myself. We had two cameras, which we set up in the hall, upon our arrival in Prague. I lit the hall as best I could with the limited lighting we had brought with us. After the concert we wrapped the gear and early the following morning were back on the train for Warsaw, and the next concert. The train rattled through the East European snow-filled landscape, while members of the orchestra chatted, played cards and slept. I saw John Ogden tirelessly practising on a silent keyboard in one of the compartments.

After the concert in Warsaw several of us including Sir John and Lady Barbirolli, and Jacqueline Dupré had dinner at the hotel's chandelier-bedecked restaurant. Two local lady violinists serenaded the Barbirollis, and I had a dance with Jacqueline Dupré who looked dazzling - a pretty special evening.

Back on the train I woke at about 4 a.m. and looked outside. The train had stopped at a large siding. A blizzard was raging and the bright overhead lights etched the falling snow against the blackness of the night. Many dark muffled figures were at work. We had reached the Russian border where (presumably for military reasons) there was a different rail gauge. In order to proceed into Russia, new bogies had to be bolted to the carriages, and the old bogies removed. All this was happening while most of the passengers were sleeping. Eventually the train moved on again bound for Moscow, and mugs of tea were served from a big samovar at the end of the corridor.

The Moscow concert was again a great success and the audience went wild. Once more Dupré had played the Elgar cello concerto and Janet Baker had sung 'Sea Pictures'. The applause was unending and from my position in the wings I filmed Barbirolli as he took his bows. The orchestra's stage manager was a cockney character called Bill. 'Only one more, Sir John,' he said after the fourth and fifth curtain calls. 'I think I'll take just *one* more,' said a happy Sir John.

The Kremlin

In June 1963 I again travelled to Moscow on the same plane as Harold Wilson, an Aeroflot jet, fitted out in Victorian décor with mock brass curtain rails and simulated red velvet curtains at the windows. He had recently become leader of the Labour party and had set up a meeting with Prime Minster Nikita Kruschev.

Since an election was coming up in just over a year's time (which he would win and become Prime Minister) he was keen on getting as much press coverage as possible.

I was covering the visit for Panorama, and it was the first time that the Kremlin had been opened to the world's press. We were looking forward to seeing art treasures never before photographed by the media, culminating in Harold Wilson entering Kruschev's office for talks. We were of course ushered out before the talks started; I then set up my camera at the entrance to the Kremlin with Wilson's car in the foreground. I thought that this would make a good shot of Harold shaking hands with Mr Kruschev, descending the magnificent steps and getting into his car.

And so it was. Wilson shook hands with Kruschev and other Russian officials at the top of the steps and headed for his car. He then spotted me and, knowing that I was filming for Panorama, he came up and said 'I'm seeing him again on Thursday'.

I nodded and said, 'I was hoping to get a shot of you getting into the car.'

'Oh sorry,' he said, 'I'll do it again'.

To my amazement he went back up the steps, shook hands with the Russian leader again, came down and entered his car. A case of history repeating itself!

Such was his desire to present himself as an ordinary working chap that on another occasion just before the Labour Party elections he wanted to be filmed for Panorama while mending his son's bike in the living room. And although he was rarely seen without the ubiquitous pipe in public, he preferred cigars when the cameras weren't present.

Hazardous Journeys

Richard Dimbleby fronted the live studio part of Panorama, as well as famously commentating on many big outside broadcast Royal events. On the two occasions I worked with him on overseas film assignments I found him immensely professional with a great sense of humour.

In the summer of 1963 King Paul of Greece was in the news. He had been criticised for interfering in local politics and he became involved in a dispute with Prime Minister Constantine Karamanlis that led to the latter's resignation, causing a certain amount of political unrest. The King and Queen had agreed to appear before the Panorama camera, to be interviewed by Richard Dimbleby.

On a stormy 2nd of July, our four-man team boarded an Olympic Airways Comet 4 flight to Athens. Shortly after taking off we encountered tremendous turbulence, there was a sudden, loud crack and we were being flung all over the sky. The cabin staff rushed to the flight deck. Among the passengers was a group of Greek Orthodox priests who fell to their knees in the aisle and started praying. The Captain came on the Tannoy to say we would be returning to London Airport, with no other explanation. Suddenly Richard Dimbleby appeared, framed in the doorway leading to the first class compartment. 'I've just had a word with the Captain', he announced to an extremely attentive audience. 'We've just lost an engine,' he said, as if it were the most natural thing in the world. 'We can fly quite happily on three, in fact we're doing it now.' The passengers applauded his calming words but in fact our troubles weren't quite over. We had to jettison most of the fuel to reduce the payload before landing back at Heathrow. Just before we did so, we were struck by lightning. Had the lightning struck whilst the fuel was streaming from the fuel tanks it might have been a different story.

Little did we know that when we finally reached Corfu we were to face another hazardous journey!

We discussed where we should film the interview with the King and Queen who were staying at the summer palace in Corfu and it was decided that the formal interview should take place in the palace gardens. I had heard that the King liked driving around Corfu in a Jeep and I suggested it would be fun to do a less formal piece on the move.

Everyone seemed to like the idea so early the next morning the King's aide was there with half the Greek Navy to assist. I had a small platform built on to the front of the Jeep just big enough to hold Grahame Whatling the soundman and myself. The Navy decided to tie us on so that there was no chance of us falling off in front of the royal wheels and causing an unseemly mess in the road.

We had been roped into place, the king was at the wheel, and the Queen sat in the front passenger seat alongside him. Richard Dimbleby was in the rear seat between the two of them. It was a wonderful set-up. Through my viewfinder I had this elegant three-shot with the mountains and glistening sea beyond.

There was a convoy of about twenty cars accompanying the Royal Jeep and I asked that it be last so that it was the only vehicle in the picture. Off we went, the Queen requesting that I would give her a thumbs up when I was filming so that she could, 'put on my Sunday face.'

Everything was going swimmingly. Richard was conducting his interview, and the King and Queen were very relaxed. As the King drove around the island we passed groups of people who politely applauded the Royal party, in accordance with the local custom. Soon we came to a spectacular coast road with stunning views. The road had a sheer drop to the sea and I noticed out of the corner of my eye that the King, preoccupied as he was with the interview, was gradually moving closer to the edge. He was bound to notice this I thought, but no he was definitely wandering towards the sheer drop.

Richard caught my eye; he had seen it too. This raised an interesting point of protocol. At what stage did one shout out 'for heaven's sake, your majesty' or words to that effect. I could see the headlines:

BBC CREW DROWNS TIED TO ROYAL LANDROVER.
KING AND QUEEN RESCUED.

The King must have sensed our concern for he finally saw what was happening, corrected his steering and we were back on course.

About to film the King of Greece driving the Panorama unit round Corfu. Left to right: Richard Dimbleby, Queen Frederica, King Paul, Grahame Whatling and N.C.

We also filmed some sailing scenes with the young crown prince, Constantine. His Karate demonstrations and brilliant mimicry of Jackie Kennedy kept us in stitches while we worked. He ascended the throne on March 6th 1964, upon the death of his father, but his brief reign was marked by political upheavals. Early in 1967 a military coup deposed the existing government and established a ruling junta, forcing him into exile.

Earthquake.

The second story I did with Richard Dimbleby, in October 1963, was very different. There had been a bad earthquake in Skopje, Macedonia. More than eleven hundred people had died and 80 per cent of the city had been destroyed. Those who were left were threatened with floods.

The four of us were sharing a tent provided by one of the relief organisations. There was a lot of water in it and like the rest of the town we were in danger of being swept away. Richard slept at the end nearest the swollen river and it was agreed that if he sailed past us during the night we would all take it as a signal to leave. He was the only one of the team who had enough common sense to bring not only brandy and instant coffee but a tiny stove on which throughout our stay he brewed the mixture and provided us all with our breakfast.

Richard Dimbleby with myself, David Webster and his assistant at the graveside of some of the victims of the disastrous earthquake in Skopje, Macedonia

I have been asked how I was affected by the suffering that I sometimes had to photograph. I am saddened when innocent people are injured or made homeless through no fault of their own, but as a professional I was there to do a job and couldn't allow my emotions to get in the way. However I would refuse to film if I thought I was intruding on private grief. Another question is, don't I want to put down my camera and help? Well yes, if there was no one else around, and direct action was needed, of course I would. But a curious thing happens when you are looking through a camera viewfinder. You feel as though you are not actually there, but are watching a picture on a screen. The lens between you and the subject insulates you from reality. In an old newsreel I saw recently on TV, filmed aboard an aircraft carrier during World War II, there was a shot of a plane landing and missing the arresting cable. It was coming straight towards the camera. The cameraman didn't try to get out of the way but continued filming until the plane hit and killed him. He was probably thinking what a sensational picture he was looking at.

With a less drastic conclusion it happened to me when I was filming at the Monte Carlo Rally in 1962. My camera position was on a hairpin bend, the place to get exciting shots. As one of the cars came hurtling round the bend, one of its wheels came off and rolled towards the camera. Looking through the viewfinder I thought, 'This is going to be a great shot'. The wheel fell on its side and came to a halt just in front of the camera. If it had gone further and hit the camera, I don't think I would have reacted until it was too late.

Norwegian Pranks

A trip to Norway on a whaling story with my friends Michael Barratt, assistant Frank Hodge and soundman John Hore, provided a little light relief. There was a two-day delay in the schedule. Frank Hodge, a practical joker was a bad influence. First there was the new microphone incident. We had to do a long list of cutaway questions (see page 21) from Michael, to be used in an interview we had shot earlier. Being a gadget freak, I had purchased a small battery razor and it looked a bit like a microphone. You can probably guess the rest. John handed it to Michael telling him it was a new radio mike. Barratt was impressed and started doing his repeat questions with gusto while speaking very seriously into the razor. I pretended to run the camera. After a while John called out 'Can you just flick that base cut switch, Mike?'

'What? Oh right,' said Michael, staring uncomprehendingly at the buzzing razor. After some delay came his usual response. 'You buggers,' he roared in his rich plum-cake voice.

The next morning while cleaning my teeth, I started to foam at the mouth. Someone had squeezed some shaving cream into my toothpaste tube.

Aswan Dam

In May 1964 Nikita Kruschev, the Russian Prime Minister, was invited by President Nasser to open the Aswan Dam in Egypt. The world's press would be there and of course so would Panorama. We flew to Cairo two days in advance, as Michael Barratt wanted to obtain an interview with President Nasser. The information office was approached with the request. 'Why not?' they said. 'Ask again tomorrow.'

The next day we tried again. 'Why not?' was the reply. 'Try tomorrow.'
'But we have to be in Aswan,' Michael protested. He received a smiling shrug.

By this time every reporter, camera crew and news photographer was in Aswan. We were still in Cairo waiting to hear about the interview. We had left it to the last possible moment before we had to abandon the attempt and go to the airport to fly

Michael Barratt doing his cutaway questions in Oslo

to Aswan for the big opening. We were greeted by bad news. The United Arab Airlines Viscount had engine trouble. There would be a delay.

'Will we be able to get there for the opening of the dam?' Michael demanded.

'Why not?' smiled an airport official.

The plane finally took off, but we were convinced we would be too late and wondered how we would explain this to Panorama editor, Paul Fox. We landed at Aswan at 11.25 a.m., five minutes before the dam was due to be opened, but we were still almost half an hour's drive away. We quickly hired a car with a driver and he was told to expect a handsome tip if he could get us there quickly.

It was a nauseating journey with screeching tyres, hairpin bends and white knuckles, the passengers instinctively stamping their right feet onto phantom brakes. Michael switched on the radio. A familiar voice was heard speaking in Russian. It was Kruschev making his opening speech. We knew that when he stopped speaking, the dam would go. The journey seemed to last an eternity but we finally juddered to a halt somewhere near the dam. Frank Hodge, my assistant grabbed the tripod, John Hore his recording gear and I the camera. We had no idea where we were. I climbed up the nearest rise and we quickly set up the camera. I pressed my eye to the viewfinder and pushed the button. With a massive roar the retaining wall of the dam was blown up and millions of gallons of water from the mighty Nile cascaded though the valley. We couldn't have chosen a better spot if we had been there days before.

That afternoon we were outside Mr Kruschev's hotel to film him emerging and getting into his car. I had by now photographed him on several occasions and had a theory that if the camera was very close to a politician, the mask would drop away and the real person would be revealed. Thus at any opportunity I could, I used a wide-angle lens and got as close as I dared - or was allowed to. For some reason Mr Kruschev's security people never stopped me although I was sometimes only a couple of feet away from the Russian leader often walking backwards as he walked forward. He never looked directly at me but I sensed a slight smile on his face on these occasions.

After he had been driven away from the hotel, presumably to fly back to Russia, we were packing our equipment when a waiter appeared with a tray of Coca-Cola. 'We didn't order this,' I said.

'Mr Kruschev sent it,' the waiter replied.

Hejaz Railway

We returned to Cairo to pursue that elusive interview. The Panorama office wanted more material to justify our airfare and Mike came up with a story on the Hejaz railway. This impressive railway ran from Turkey through Syria, Jordan and Saudi Arabia and had been built to carry pilgrims to Mecca. It was largely destroyed during the First World War by Lawrence's marauding Arabs, because of its role as a supply-line for the Turks. This was depicted in the David Lean film *Lawrence of Arabia*. The three countries planned a joint venture to rebuild it. This was a complicated project to film and, to cover more ground, we split our team. Michael and Frank took the spare camera to Jordan while John and I hired a Cessna to fly along the railway track in the Saudi Arabian desert, which I reckoned would produce some pretty spectacular pictures. The pilot of the Cessna skilfully flew the plane at fifty feet or so above the ground and with the camera pointing out of the window we had some good shots of the railway track flashing past. Suddenly he increased his height.

'What's happened?' I asked.

'We're about to pass an encampment,' he said. 'I've gone up to make it more difficult for them to take pot shots at us.'

'Why would they want to do that?' I asked. He shrugged. Some questions do not have answers.

We were to end our journey by landing at the holy city of Jeddah where our Muslim pilot, thought we could get some good pictures. When the Cessna landed and taxied to a halt we were immediately surrounded by three jeeps full of turbaned, robed and heavily armed guards.

I swung out of the plane and gave them a friendly 'Hallo!' The leader of the gang responded with a less than friendly '*Goodbye*'.

We were informed that as infidels we were forbidden to enter the holy city. The guards ordered us in no uncertain manner to return to the Cessna and fly off, or be arrested.

There were many more problems before we completed this story: midnight border incidents, threats and passport irregularities. Michael Barratt describes these in detail in his book, *Michael Barratt by Michael Barratt.* And we failed to obtain our interview with President Nasser.

A Question of Questions

I worked on Panorama for three years and not all of the stories were political. Elizabeth Taylor and Richard Burton were appearing at the Oxford Playhouse in *Who's afraid of Virginia Wolf.* Reporter Kenneth Allsop, a friend of theirs, was to do a rare interview with them.

They turned up at a location in Putney Hill. It was evening and I had arranged two chairs in front of some partly-open French windows, with the flimsy curtains gently moving in the breeze. I naturally took great care over the lighting and they both looked like a million dollars. Kenneth did his interview, which took about half an hour, and afterwards they disappeared. We then set up for Allsop's cutaway questions. He was about half way through when a voice said, 'You didn't ask me that.' It was Elizabeth, who was listening in the shadows.

'I did Liz,' said Kenneth, 'I have them all written down'. She murmured something and swept out of the room.

Because the questions were filmed again afterwards it was possible for an unscrupulous reporter (which Allsop was *not*) to alter the question to give a different meaning to the already recorded answer. For instance if someone was asked 'how would you eat poached eggs?' and they replied 'I'd have them on toast', and afterwards the question was changed to 'What should be done about endangered species?', the answer 'I'd have them on toast' would be construed in an entirely different way.

The producer and Kenneth went back to Lime Grove, and we were wrapping the camera, lights and sound, when Burton stormed in and grabbed me by the lapels almost yanking me off my feet. He was flushed with anger.

'Where's Allsop?' he demanded. I was truthfully able to say that he had left the building. There was an exasperated pause and he stormed out; I was in no doubt that the incident would soon be forgotten. I never did find out what Liz objected to about that particular question.

Baptism by Fire

The camera room at Ealing was just across the corridor from the viewing theatres. There were eight little rooms each with a few cinema seats and a small screen. These were all serviced from a large projection area running along the rear of the theatres. The projectionists were young enthusiasts who wanted eventually, to work in the camera department and were all waiting for a vacancy. It was a standing joke that if a projectionist handed you a cup of coffee, you should check it for arsenic first. On this occasion one of them, Mark, came into the camera room looking for me. 'Ken Russell's in theatre four,' he said nonchalantly, 'watching some of your Panorama stories.' My butterflies started performing the Dance of the Hours. I slipped into the projection area and looked through the glazed projection port of theatre four. Sure enough on the screen were my Liz Taylor and Richard Burton pictures. I couldn't make out who was viewing it.

The Ealing lighting and camera crews are setting up a studio shot for an Arts programme. The electricians carry gloves to protect their hands while handling the hot lighting equipment. I can't remember the significance of the object of our attention. Hardly Henry Moore!

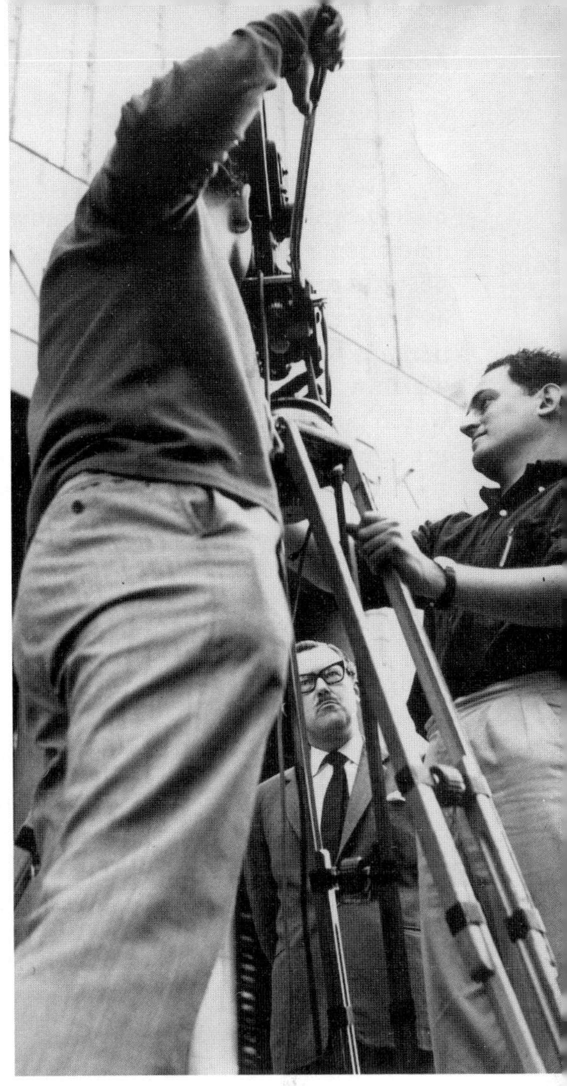

Clockwise:
Harold Macmillan at Chequers for Panorama:
Whicker's World U.S.A.:
A blind dog story For Blue Peter

Although I had enjoyed my years as a current affairs cameraman, working mainly on Panorama, it occurred to me after a while that maybe there were only about ten events that could happen to the world and I began to feel as if I had been there before. I had always wanted to photograph dramas. I felt that working, as a director of photography on screenplays would offer new challenges, enable me perhaps to use my imagination more, to work in a world of illusions, the events of which were written and acted. Even if the dramas were based on real events, they weren't real, only appeared to be real, a world away from the daily routine of predictable and usually depressing news headlines.

Once you had been branded as a documentary cameraman it was difficult to get work in the drama department. It was a separate and exclusive world; drama producers seemed rarely to watch reportage or at least didn't feel that it had much relevance to their work.

A few days later I was called to a meeting with director Ken Russell and told that I was to shoot his film, *Dante's Inferno*. Apparently I was chosen because his regular cameraman, Dick Bush, was ill.

I found this exciting news. It would be a radical change of lifestyle and thought process. I visited the library and did some research. *Dante's Inferno* is a film drama about the Pre-Raphaelites, the group of nineteenth-century English painters, poets and critics who rebelled against the art of the day. The Pre-Raphaelite Brotherhood was established in 1848 and its central figure was the painter and poet Dante Gabriel Rossetti. The main thrust of the film is the tempestuous relationship between Gabriel Rossetti and artist's model, Lizzie Siddons, culminating in her suicide from an overdose of laudanum. Rossetti discovers her body when he returns home from one of his binges. He is distraught and full of remorse and at the funeral places his new book of poems in the coffin. Eight years later, having recovered from the loss of Lizzie, he enlists the help of some shady friends, to open the grave and recover the poems.

This was to be the first scene we were to shoot. About midnight a coffin was placed in a grave that had been dug by the props department. Inside the coffin was a dummy of Lizzie produced by the Special Effects Department. I thought the dummy looked pretty convincing but Ken did not.

'Where's Judith?' he demanded. Judith Paris was the actress playing Lizzie Siddons.

'It's her night off, Ken, she'll be asleep,' said the first assistant director.

'I don't care, get her down here,' said Ken. Poor Judith was sleepily bundled into a taxi and rushed to the set. There she had to spend an hour being made up to look like someone who had been buried for eight years. Ken was finally satisfied. The coffin was to be hauled to the surface with ropes operated by Gabriel's villainous accomplices, then he would force the coffin open with a pickaxe remove the lid and retrieve the book of poems. Gabriel Rossetti was played by Oliver Reed, who else?

To get an overhead shot I hand-held the camera while standing astride the grave and shooting down into it. Ken wanted the scene to be lit entirely with flaming torches held by the actors, an idea I liked very much. Judith, shivering in her shroud in the cold night air and looking decidedly unwell, climbed into the coffin and was lowered into the grave while Oliver Reed and the other actors had their torches ignited by prop men. Ken Russell wielded a flaming torch too, just for the hell of it. On 'action' the coffin was raised. In the flickering torchlight Oliver Reed brutally opened the coffin with his pickaxe, gazed for a poignant moment at the corpse and with a heavy heart retrieved the book. Meanwhile Ken was leaping around gesticulating with his flare, yelling instructions to the actors. I was filming astride the grave when I noticed flames coming from between my legs! It was Ken getting over excited with his flaming torch. I decided it would be prudent to wear a flameproof nappy for the rest of the takes.

Working with Ken Russell was a revelation. I learnt a lot from his strong visual sense and his eye for offbeat compositions; in fact I regard him as my mentor. His operatic rages were without malice and no one could possibly have taken offence at them.

After we had finished the film I received invitations to several of his parties. He used to set up a projector and show some of his favourite cinematic moments. I remember one hilarious 'Food Flash' made during or just after the war. There were two ladies with frightfully refined accents demonstrating to the working classes how to make a cup of tea. 'Draw the water freshly from the well,' they advised.

Cockney Pride

In 1966 I worked for a while on a programme called Whole Scene Going.

It was a sort of forerunner to Top of the Pops but also contained film stories about the personalities and actors of the entertainment world. I remember spending a few fun days in Paris shooting zany footage with Dave Dee, Beaky, Mick and Tich, a boy band that was popular at the time. On another occasion we interviewed a young actor who had just completed a film. We did his interview on a boat so that we could see the south side of the Thames as he reminisced about his childhood in South London. The film was *Alfie* and the actor was a young Michael Caine.

That evening we filmed at the *Alfie* end-of-production party, which took place at the Cockney Pride in Piccadilly. The cast and crew were there including Michael Caine, Shelly Winters, Millicent Martin, Jane Asher and Denholm Elliot. Among the other guests were singers Lulu and Cilla Black who had sung the haunting 'What's it all about Alfie?' over the opening credits. The Beatles, whom I had worked with before, were also there. There was a good atmosphere and everyone looked relaxed. I started to film, wandered up and down the room, my hand-held camera roaming continuously over the celebrities in the style of *cinema verité*. Every time I approached Paul McCartney he would jokingly put his hand over my lens. Of course this made me approach him frequently, and the hand over the lens became a running gag. I also filmed Lulu coming out of a door marked 'Loo'. I don't thing anyone else got the joke but it made me laugh.

The Fab Four

Blues

Colour Television is today taken for granted, but all of the programmes I have described above were shot in black and white.

In July 1967 the BBC started transmitting in colour. At Ealing shooting on black and white film ceased and early in 1967 we changed to colour. Cameramen were sent on a week's course to the BBC training centre at Evesham, which made a pleasant change from the usual routine. I had recently acquired a second hand Alfa Romeo Veloce, and had an exhilarating trip to Evesham one glorious Sunday morning on the new and empty M40 Motorway.

In the past the BBC had supplied black and white Radio Rental television sets to staff who needed to monitor the quality of their work, but supplying colour sets was considered far too expensive for this practice to continue. Since few people then could afford colour sets, one of the only ways to see your work being transmitted in colour was to go to the TV Centre in White City and watch it on a colour monitor. This was not ideal as it was a rather long journey from where I was living at the time. However there was another way. Not far from where I lived was a Radio Rentals shop sporting a massive colour TV set in the window. That night it was raining heavily as I stood in the street watching the transmission of my first colour film, an Arts programme shot in Ireland, through the rain-spattered shop window. Who said working in television was glamorous?

James Cameron

In January of 1967 I was to work on a documentary directed by Richard Marquand called *Point of Departure,* based on the first chapter of James Cameron's book of the same name.

I read the book and found this opening chapter extremely moving, dealing as it did with his life as a fledgling journalist in Dundee, the loss of his wife in childbirth, his unhappy second marriage and the death of his beloved father. Later of course, he was to become a highly respected journalist renowned for his compassion and integrity as well as the quality of his writing.

James and I hit it off right from the start. I found him easy to talk to and he seemed to admire what little talent I had been given as an image-gatherer. We had many late-night conversations in the hotel bars of Hong Kong, Singapore and Dundee. We did several documentaries together in a series called *Cameron's Country* but I think the high spot for me was a film on the aircraft carrier H.M.S. *Eagle*.

James Cameron (left), Director Richard Marquand and N.C. enjoying hospitality aboard the *Eagle*

On the morning of Wednesday 13th March we were about to depart from a base in Singapore in a navy helicopter whose mission was to locate *Eagle* sailing somewhere in the China Sea and land a BBC film crew on her deck.

We all clambered aboard the helicopter with some anticipation of the exciting trip that lay ahead. The pilot appeared and started to brief us.

'When we ditch,' he said, as if there was no alternative, 'there is a temptation to immediately get out. Don't. The rotors will still be revolving and they will cut your head off. Wait for me to get out when I think it is safe. Now as the water starts coming up to your chest there is a temptation to take a big breath. Don't. Wait till the water is up to your chin, and then take a breath. Now it's dark, you're under the water, how are you going to find your way out?'

No one had an answer, not even James. 'Well it's simple,' he said, 'run your hand round this rail and feel the way the plastic arrows are pointing until you come to the door.'

We took off and some 40 minutes later the *Eagle* appeared, looking magnificent as she ploughed through a glittering sea. We landed on her deck, were given a warm welcome and shown to our quarters. The filming was to take about a week.

Surely there can be few more exciting places than the flight deck of an aircraft carrier. When filming at airports a cameraman is not allowed to get very close to moving aircraft, but here, they are taking off and landing within a few feet of you. We were assigned an officer to look after us and he used to hold me by the scruff of the neck when I was shooting, so that I was able to get in really close. Just before a plane was to be steam-catapulted into the sky, crouched with my eye to the camera, he would firmly drag me back to a safe position. Because of his expertise I was able to get some really exciting shots.

While we were on board I wanted to do some helicopter shots of the *Eagle* steaming through the seas. The pilot was brilliant and was able to place the helicopter anywhere I asked him and a few places I hadn't! We did one shot almost at sea level with the ship steaming straight towards us. At the last minute the pilot swooped towards the sky and swung round enabling me to get a beautiful top shot of *Eagle*. 'That was great,' I gasped through the intercom. 'The Old Man's going to kill me for that one,' came the response. After doing several other shots a garbled message suddenly came though my headset and we dropped like a stone. I hastily tried to remember the briefing. Don't get out before the rotors have stopped, don't breath until the water's up to your chin...follow the plastic arrows. My panic was short-lived. Our descent stopped a few feet from the surface of the China Sea. There I saw a huge whale looking up at us, curious about the strange thing hovering above him. The message from the pilot that I had not understood was 'Do you want a shot of the whale?'

When we had finished the *Eagle* film, we flew to Hong Kong to do another film about the 'Susie Wong' bar area, which was being redeveloped.

Several years after the series was completed, James was travelling in India on an assignment and was being driven at high speed by a local driver. Most of the Indian trunk roads had a very narrow strip of tarmac and one or other of on-coming vehicles had to give way by moving to the dusty verges. A bus was hurtling towards James' car. Both drivers were determined that the other should move aside. There was a horrendous crash and James was very badly injured.

A beautiful Indian nurse looked after him in hospital and they fell in love and married. Although he never completely recovered from the accident, he told me this was the happiest time of his life. I worked with him again in Israel and his wife was there too. She was always by his side until his death a few years later.

Return to the River Kwai

In October 1968 I was to work on two documentaries back to back. The first was on the Thai-Burmese border.

The feature film *Bridge on the River Kwai* depicted the terrible hardships suffered by British prisoners of war captured during the Japanese occupation of Thailand and Burma in the Second World War. Although the Alec Guinness character was fictional, the situation was real enough. The prisoners were put to work building the Siam-Burma Railway in temperatures of 100 degrees in the shade. There were reports of interrogations and beatings, inadequate food and lack of medical supplies. One in three men perished.

We returned to the River Kwae Noi to give it its real name with ex-POW John Coast who had written a book about his experiences. Tony de Lotbinière directed the film for the *One Pair of Eyes* series. The plan was to fly the former Commandant of the POW camp from Japan to the site of the camp, where the two men were to confront each other.

It was a strange situation with the ex-Commandant, now a mild-mannered Tokyo bank manager, facing John at the derelict Kanburi camp. There were still some remains of huts although the surrounding jungle had erased much. John and the Commandant wandered around trying to recognise certain areas, and it was obviously an emotional experience for both of them.

It was in fact a rather friendly meeting. John thought that some of the reports of atrocities had been exaggerated, and was fairly satisfied with his treatment by the Japanese authorities. Others perhaps had a different experience. I have just been reading Eric Lomax's *The Railway Man*, which contains horrific accounts of beatings and torture.

Later we waited to take pictures of a train approaching. We sat quietly for 30 minutes or so with the camera and sound ready. Then there was a distant and eerie shrieking whistle echoing round the steeply wooded valley before the train at last came into view, hugging the hillside and moving precariously along a creaking wooden embankment that had been built at such cost. I remembered my sister-in-law's brother who had died on that railway project.

Bali Dance

After shooting was completed in Thailand, Tony de Lotbinière flew back to London taking the film rushes with him. The rest of us, my assistant Keith Burton, soundman Roger Turner and electrician Tony Thorpe, took the plane from Bangkok to Bali, where David Attenborough was to join us. We were to shoot a documentary for the Music and Arts department about Balinese dancing.

On the drive from Bali Airport to our hotel I was struck by the complete absence of the ugly sprawling industrial wasteland that usually drapes airport highways. Here there was a succession of neat villages sited in courtyards behind beautifully carved archways and interspersed with small soapstone temples again all intricately carved with images of Hindu Gods. As we drove past, bursts of percussive music could be heard from the gamelan orchestras, that each village seemed to have. The hillsides were embossed with irrigated, terraced rice fields and we passed a boy leading a procession of ducks in single file; trained to follow the white flag he was holding aloft.

At this time David Attenborough occupied the exalted position of Controller of BBC2. In spite of the demands of his post, the call of the wild became impossible for him to ignore. He took three weeks leave, shed his pinstripes and donned his safari suit once more and joined us in Bali. I had worked with David before, but I was a little worried that now that he had achieved these dizzy executive heights I would have to treat him differently. There was no need for my concern. When he arrived from London in a flurry of enthusiasm, he was his usual chummy and delightful self and very glad to be back in the real world.

The dance tradition of Bali has flourished and evolved for 1000 years. The walled village of Pietan, famous for the quality of its dancers was to be our main location. We filmed there nearly every day and sometimes at night during spectacular performances. We looked at the training of young girls by the elder women of the village and the performances of more accomplished dancers, accompanied by the stirring gamelan village orchestra. These dancers and musicians were not simple village folk. Many had performed in London, Rome, Paris and New York but they were always glad to return to the rural life of their beloved island.

It seems that the Balinese had learnt how to accept tourism without letting it encroach on their everyday life. Areas designated for tourists persuaded the visitors that they were seeing the true Bali, while life went on relatively undisturbed for the village population. This was in 1968 I don't know if it is the same today.

The village was about two hours' drive from the Bali Beach Hotel built for tourists and incongruously divorced from the surrounding architecture like a huge white ship at anchor. We had hired two land rovers with drivers, to carry our equipment and us.

Travelling around the world with about thirty large cases of baggage was a sometimes irksome but necessary part of the job. In this case since we were carrying lights for the night filming, we had even more cases than usual. Arrivals and departures from Airports were always an anxious time. Just one case going astray could seriously hold up filming on our inevitably tight schedules. Local Customs officers examined everything. They checked that the documents we carried accurately listed the contents of each package, before they would release the equipment. Customs officers in India were particularly vigilant and carried out the British-taught procedures meticulously. As a young assistant I once spent five hours arguing and pleading with officials in a customs shed at Delhi Airport in a temperature of 113 degrees. They wanted the BBC to pay something like £10,000 in import duty although our equipment should have been regarded as a temporary importation and therefore not liable to duty. The rest of the team had long since departed to their air-conditioned hotel, and I felt a great sense of achievement when, after much cajolery, the equipment was finally released to me, duty free. No such problems had been encountered at Bali Airport.

Temples

Daily filming proceeded at the village. The inhabitants were friendly and quick to accept us, although we must have seemed like a strange blot on their highly carved, gilded and beautiful landscape. The lengthy journey back to the hotel at the end of the day would be enlivened by David leading us in community singing, much to the amusement of the Balinese drivers.

After a meal, when we weren't working in the evenings, we would listen to David's entertaining stories of previous adventures. There was the time when he had to purchase mules to cross a desert. This was duly noted on his expense claim. At the end of the journey he sold them again, as was the local practice. The admin office in London pointed out that staff were not allowed to sell BBC property. He was ordered to return the mules to the stores at TV Centre. He finally resolved this dilemma by saying that he couldn't return them as his team had eaten them.

The Balinese would often convert an area of natural wonder into a temple. For instance there was a place at the foot of steep cliffs where hundreds of turtles gathered. This had been designated a turtle temple. On a previous trip to Bali David had filmed at a bat temple. He mentioned that this was one of the most unpleasant places he had ever visited and that we wouldn't be going back there on this trip. I was curious but he didn't elaborate.

Mountain ranges cross Bali from East to West and the highest point is Mt Agung, a volcano that erupted in March 1963. In these mountain regions a different kind of dance took place, known as spirit dancing. It was performed mainly by men and very little was known about this by Westerners. We planned to visit this remote region and to film at a village where spirit dancing was taking place. It was a difficult journey that would take many hours. A large part of it, without roads, involved driving up volcanic larva slopes.

After about two hours of climbing, the land rovers reached a small village. David with a twinkle in his eye, said that this was the location of the bat temple, and did I feel like taking a few shots? We unpacked the camera and sound and a battery light and made our way to the entrance of a cave. The temperature outside was in the high 90s but as I stepped inside there was a wall of overpowering heat. Tony the electrician switched on his battery light flooding the interior with light and I saw the reason for the sudden increase in the temperature. The roof of the large cave was thick with bats, millions of them. The noise was deafening and their droppings were raining down like a tropical storm. In spite of the heat I put on a plastic mac and a hat and went further into the cave. The floor was about a two feet thick with bat droppings. Walking on it was quite disgusting. On the surface and feeding voraciously, was a seething mass of cockroaches. And there in front of me feeding on the cockroaches were two large pythons. I raised my camera and began shooting. When I came to shoot close-ups of the pythons they were quite still. 'It's a pity they're not moving,' I said to David. 'Hang on,' he said, and found a piece of wood. He gently prodded one of the snakes and it reared up magnificently. We finished the filming, retreated and I threw away my soiled mac and hat. Outside it seemed wonderfully cool after the heat and the stench. I thought I noticed that the drivers weren't their usual smiling selves; in fact they seemed quite worried. We climbed back into the land rovers and continued our journey.

Hours later, as dusk was approaching, we entered the village of Iseh where the spirit dancing was to take place. The villagers gathered and began chanting while the dancers inhaled the smoke of some sort of hallucinogenic herb. I couldn't help feeling that the scene was reminiscent of a Hollywood movie and I almost expected Dorothy Lamour to appear at any moment.

One dancer thought he was a horse and pranced around alarmingly like a wild stallion. Another became a pot lid and rushed around looking for a pot to put his lid on. Tony was holding the battery light and the dancer mistook it for a pot and thumped it, invoking a stream of cockney expletives! These dancers were in a trance and were surrounded by the villagers to prevent them leaving the village. We were told that one dancer who became a pig, had escaped, and was found days later eating his own excrement.

It was quite late when filming was completed and we were to stay that night in a nearby house that the owner had kindly vacated. When we arrived we found that an elaborate cold meal had been prepared for us, which we all devoured with enthusiasm. Balinese food is very highly spiced and some of it is so hot that it makes a vindaloo curry taste bland by comparison.

The next morning everyone, except David Attenborough, was very ill with a fever, diarrhoea and vomiting. Tony said afterwards that I told him I thought I was dying although I don't remember saying it. I was shivering in spite of the heat and he covered me with a Mylar space blanket. Since none of us, apart from David was fit to work, we were bundled into one of the land rovers to be taken back to the hotel. The driver chose to go down the other side of the mountain to our approach, as it was a shorter route.

We had left a battery belt behind at the bat temple and David said that he would take the other land rover back the way we had come, to retrieve it.

We set off, David in one direction, the rest of us in the other. The four of us were sprawling in the vehicle; feeling very ill, and being bounced around on the rough terrain. I don't remember how much time had passed but suddenly I sat up. Everyone else was doing the same. The fever had left us as suddenly as it had come. By the time we had reached the hotel we were all fully recovered. David arrived and was surprised to find us hale and hearty.

He had a strange story. When he and the driver had arrived at the bat temple to collect the battery belt, the driver handed him a little basket of flowers and motioned David to kneel. The driver then said a prayer. He explained that it was considered extremely blasphemous to touch a sacred python and although it was David who had touched the snake, it had been done at my bidding. As far as we could tell, it was at that moment that the fever had left us during our journey on the other side of the mountain.

Back at Piatan, having completed our filming, the village threw a farewell party for us with a sumptuous feast. This time there were no after effects. It was sad saying goodbye to all the friends we had made and knowing that we would probably never meet them again. We drove away with the familiar sounds of the gamelan fading into the distance.

Holiday Visit

I was still a bachelor. I had had one or two relationships but my travels usually prevented them from developing. Anyway I didn't seem to be very good at maintaining long-term partnerships, but was perfectly happy as I was. I have always been a bit of a loner and do not mind my own company.

My mother had died and my dad was living with me at a house I had bought near to my married sister. This meant that she and my brother-in-law could keep an eye on my father, a sprightly 80, while I was away. I had a boat on the River Crouch and during voyages to the estuary my father was often my sailing companion. He enjoyed this new life and I came across him one day studying a book on navigation.

Then there was the time when my dad met Patrick Moore. I had been working with Patrick on a documentary based on several letters he had received from people with rather startling views about our solar system - ideas that couldn't actually be disproved. There was a man who spoke fluent Venutian. We interviewed him and the sounds that he produced were indeed extraordinary. There was another man who had constructed a revolutionary telescope out of a roll of lino, which he claimed could give him close-up view of activities on Mars.

One of our contributors, a man who had convincingly argued that the moon was made out of asphalt, lived fairly close to me. So I invited the unit including Patrick, to come to my house for a quick lunch before filming. By this time we had been filming for two weeks or more and were all good friends. I had made a big pot of leek and potato soup and everyone tucked in, including of course my dad. At one point I noticed that my dad and Patrick were in a corner having an earnest conversation. I could see that my dad, his eyes shining, could hardly believe that he, a simple tailor, was talking to Patrick Moore. They seem to be getting on famously and it was with some reluctance that I had to suggest that it was time to do some work.

A few days after this event, I was having a day off filming to read a script.

There was a knock at the door. I opened it to reveal a rather shy and pretty girl. Her name was Anne and she was a distant relative from Auckland in New Zealand. She was having a short holiday in England and an aunt of mine who had been holidaying in New Zealand, had suggested that Anne should visit my dad. She was staying at a hostel in London, and when I said that she was welcome to stay at the house for the remainder of her holiday, she accepted. The holiday was intended to be for three more weeks but in fact she stayed for fifteen years.

Mad Jack

Anne was a bit star-struck, so I took her with me to the location of the film I was working on at the time.

Directed by Jack Gold for the *Play for Today* series, *Mad Jack* was a screenplay set in the First World War. It was based on a true story of Siegfried Sassoon an officer and a poet who, while fighting at the front, protested at the needless casualties caused by inefficient administration. The authorities ignored his protests. In fact eventually he became an embarrassment and was sent to Craig Lockhart, a mental hospital for the military. Jack Hedly played Sassoon. A set, consisting of army HQ huts and the trenches had been built on Stage 3A at Ealing Studios and the battle scenes were filmed there and on location near Weymouth. For the battle scenes many of the extras had to look wounded and maimed and often dead.

The make-up supervisor Sandra Shepherd and her colleagues were in their element. Don't ask me why but make-up girls who are usually kind, friendly and bubbly, are never happier than when creating blood and gore. Simulate an amputation? They love it. Like just one eye? No problem. To discover an actor eating a jam donut at the catering wagon, while covered in realistic looking blood, with vital parts of his body missing, is enough to put you off your bacon sandwich.

We had three weeks of studio work on the film. I had known director Jack Gold since his Tonight days as a production assistant. In common with many other directors, he could get very tense as the filming progressed. He had just completed a feature film, *The Bofors Gun*, and complained that the studio discipline at Ealing was not as good as on a feature set. Having now worked on features, I am inclined to agree with him. On one particular day there were a lot people in the studio: extras, actors, production staff, make up, lighting crew, props, grips, costume, camera crew, sound crew and design teams. When the red light was on and the bell had been sounded, everyone had to remain quiet for a rehearsal or a take. Jack gave us all a lecture on our poor studio discipline. We all stood in silence listening dutifully. 'Someone is still whispering,' yelled Jack. We all strained our ears scarcely breathing. 'I can still hear it,' he said. 'I want absolute silence or else they can get out.' The silence could now almost be felt. Jack was having a bad day and he was still angry and accusing. Suddenly a voice was heard coming from the lighting rail high above the studio floor. Doing a very bad Sinatra impersonation, the voice crooned 'Scoobie Doobie Doo, strangers in the night.' It was an electrician who had not heard the bell and was not aware of the drama going on below him. Everyone laughed, even Jack as I recall.

Mad Jack was a powerful piece of drama and was awarded a Prix Italia.

Kip

After Anne came Kip. He was of muscular build and usually wore a grin. He had a habit of creeping up on you when least expected, and giving you a big kiss. He was equally capable of engaging you in a wrestling match, which he usually won with an affectionate bite. Kip was an English bull terrier or should that read 'bull terror'? When Anne had come to stay and said she liked dogs, I was able to fulfil a long-held ambition. With so much travelling it had been impossible to have a dog but Anne said she was happy to look after Kip when I was abroad. When I felt like doing my Bill Sykes impression, he often stayed with me in my Volkswagen motor caravan, which I now preferred to a hotel, especially on dramas. I am very fond of my colleagues, but mingling with fifty or so people round a hotel bar every night after working with them all day, was not my idea of relaxing. Kip, my first dog, became well known to the film crews of Ealing and further a-field. He quickly became familiar with the movie scene and made it his business to know every one of the fifty or so members of a drama unit. He would go around checking them and if a stranger arrived he would bark at them, which could be embarrassing for me especially if it happened to be the executive producer. It seemed that having a dog like Kip on location was good for morale and there was no shortage of volunteers to look after him. I popped into the make-up caravan on one occasion to find Kip sitting there wearing his usual grin, being fondled by three make-up ladies. Some dogs have all the luck.

Mal de mer

It was January 1970 and three colleagues and I were on a 747 Jumbo to Santiago to shoot a film in the World About Us series. The subject was a look at the land behind Cape Horn, Tierra del Fuego. We found it an extremely wild and windy place. The wind was so strong that we could lean at a crazy angle into it without falling over. We were based at Punta Arenas, the last town before Antarctica.

There is a Welsh community, descendants of the missionaries of the nineteenth century. We filmed at a remote sheep farm; the only practical access being by means of the Cessna aircraft that the son of the Welsh-speaking family operated. When we had finished filming on the farm, he was ready to ferry us back to Punta Arenas. Because of the limited space it took two trips and I waited at the farm for the Cessna to return. For once the wind had dropped, the sun was shining and I lay in a field enjoying the deep peace. A flock of birds flew high overhead and I could clearly hear their wings flapping. I had never before or since experienced such silence.

Back at Punta Arenas we prepared for another journey. We were to sail round Cape Horn in a tug with the Chilean Navy. To tell the truth I was not entirely looking forward to the experience. I am not a great sailor although the Film Operations Manager at Ealing seemed to think that I was. The myth was born when as an assistant; I was offered the chance to shoot for three weeks on a White Sea-bound trawler as an acting cameraman - just producer Tim Slessor and me. Obviously it would have been crazy to turn down an opportunity like that and in spite of bouts of seasickness I got the story and the seafaring reputation. I was then given an assignment on a drifter, wallowing in the North Sea for 24 hours. The director, Ron Smedley who had been on the drifter during a recce, decided not to accompany us and gave me a long list of shots he needed. My assistant, John Wyatt and myself were both seasick but not at the same time. One of us would grab the camera and shoot before succumbing. The myth was perpetuated.

The Chilean Navy was to accommodate us on their patrol tug *Lientur.* We were to sail through the Beagle Channel, wait for the weather, and then make a run for it round the Horn.

The voyage through the Beagle Channel was beautiful with scudding clouds that changed the light every few seconds, making the glacier glint in the flickering sun. That evening, Sunday 1st February 1970, we dropped anchor in Alan Gardener Bay since there were no sheltered harbours. The wind was force 10, quite normal for that part of the world. I had a pretty unpleasant night being thrown out of my bunk several times by the ship's violent movement. Feeling ill I staggered to the heads and lay with my arms anchored round the lavatory bowl. In between bouts of seasickness my thoughts became philosophical. I wondered what I was doing there and mused on whether my career was taking the right direction.

I was awakened the next morning after a brief sleep, by the smell of baking bread and my spirits revived. There was a crew of about thirty men and four officers and having us on board seemed to be a welcome change for them. I asked the Chief Engineer what weather we could expect when rounding the Horn. 'I hope it is better than this,' he said, 'otherwise we shall all be feeding the fishes.'

We eventually reached the estuary and the weather was assessed for our entry into the open seas. The wind was force 6 and the Captain decided that it was as good as it would get and he ordered 'Full ahead both'.

Cape Horn had earned its stormy reputation by being situated at the meeting point of three oceans, the Atlantic Ocean, the Antarctic Ocean and the Pacific Ocean. It was an awe-inspiring sight. The scale of the gigantic waves was beyond belief and in the vast seas the tug seemed Lilliputian. I remembered the seafarer's prayer that begins, 'Oh Lord, the sea is so big and my ship is so small'.

I seemed to have gained my sea legs and began to feel better. I was of course there to do a job, and that does focus the mind. I had to wedge myself against a winch in order to be able to stand upright, and two crew members hung on to me to prevent me from going overboard as I held the camera.

When filming at sea it is best to try to keep the horizon steady and let the ship move in and out of the frame. If the camera were mounted on a tripod, the wildness of the sea wouldn't be so apparent There is in fact a special tripod that will keep the camera level, whatever the ship is doing. It is extremely heavy and beyond the scope of a small documentary unit, to carry such equipment.

I noticed that the Chief Engineer was 'feeding the fishes' as he had predicted. No one seemed completely immune from seasickness. Most ships steered through the Strait of Magellan as a way of avoiding this trio of merging oceans. Since this was a navy patrol vessel they had to do things the hard way. That evening we arrived in Alsina Bay where we were to spend the night. The waves were much quieter as we climbed aboard the small whaler that the ship carried, and chugged off to explore some caves. We were also able to take distant shots of *Lientur*. The captain obligingly steamed back and forth for my camera before finally anchoring.

We arrived at Porto William at 7 p.m. the next evening and disembarked, feeling unsteady on the apparently heaving land. We accompanied the captain and some of the crew to a local hostelry for a farewell drink.

So often in this job you would meet people, sometimes in hazardous or demanding conditions, and for a few days or weeks you would become close friends. Then the work was over and in all likelihood; you would never meet again. We flew back to Punta Arenas in a DC3, faster but hardly less turbulent.

The Birds

On the 3rd March 1971 I met one of the great directors of the cinema, Alfred Hitchcock. He was to be interviewed in his hotel suite at London's Claridges. We had set up the camera; but when the great man appeared there was a problem. A road drill had started in the street outside making it almost impossible to record good sound. Someone was despatched to ask the workmen to stop for half an hour and whilst this was happening, we talked. He was very approachable and seemed more than willing to discuss his films. I asked him about a shot that had been puzzling me for ages. It was in *The Birds*. A girl runs into a phone box to make a call for help and seagulls are attacking the phone box trying to get in. I asked Mr Hitchcock how this was done. 'Very simple,' he said in his sepulchral voice 'we catapulted them in.'

I doubt whether this method would be allowed today, and with the computer technology now available, it would hardly be necessary anyway.

There's a Small Hotel

In the Ealing canteen on a 'standby' day, a group of us were having a discussion about our best and worst meals, best and worst hotels etc.

I remembered my best meal as being the rather unlikely combination of guillemot's eggs, tinned sardines, stale bread, rancid butter and Bergen brandy. It was when I had been assisting Dougie Wolfe doing a story for Tonight with reporter Macdonald Hastings. We had been filming wildlife on the Lofoten Islands in the Norwegian Sea and were in a small boat crossing the Vestfjorden back to our base on the mainland. It was 3 a.m. and, being summer, bright daylight. We suddenly became aware that we hadn't eaten anything all day. As we chugged across the silvery water our Norwegian guide produced a small spirit stove, the eggs, bread, sardines, butter and brandy. No starred restaurant could have produced anything more delicious.

The worst hotel was not difficult to recall. In April 1961 we were on a car journey in the Punjab, in north-west India. It was the hot season and the temperature was 120 degrees, too hot to have the car windows open in our non-air-conditioned vehicle, because of the searing blast of heat off the road. Our objective was to film scenes depicting the judicial system in three remote villages. Each village made us extraordinarily welcome, putting on displays, providing us with interesting beverages, and garlanding us with flowers and their accompanying insects. After we had filmed and as soon as we could politely do so, we left for the next village some distance away. Again more hospitality, gym displays and garlands, then back to our travelling oven for the final village. Several hours later we arrived at the hotel that we had been booked into for the night, The New Roxy Hotel, Jelundra. The bedrooms were the size of a prison cell each one equipped with a large revolving fan designed to push the searingly-hot air back down again. The temperature during the night was 113 degrees and every half-hour or so I stood under the 'cold' shower, itself the temperature of a hot bath. Eventually we all emerged into the open courtyard and decided we had to sleep outside. The manager reluctantly had five wooden camp beds arranged on the roof. This was some improvement, but our joy was short lived. The beds were full of bed bugs, which emerged to enjoy their unexpected meal.

I may not return to the New Roxy Hotel, Jelundra. I wonder what the old Roxy was like?

Ascent of Man

When I was very young there was a radio programme called The Brains Trust featuring a group of learned men and women who would answer listeners' questions. I remember being impressed by the range of knowledge and wisdom that the team possessed. Two of the stars were Professor Joad and Doctor Bronowski. Joad had a high-pitched professorial voice, Bronowski spoke deliberately and earnestly, with a faint East European accent.

In March 1971 I was to work on a major documentary series about the history of science. It was to be called the *Ascent of Man* and Doctor Jacob Bronowski was to be the writer and narrator. Thirteen programmes were planned, each running for fifty minutes, and shooting was going to take approximately one year. There were to be two camera crews, my ex-assistant John Else heading one and I the other. The two crews would be in different parts of the world and Dr Bronowski would fly between them accompanied by executive producer Adrian Malone, to narrate his material to camera. While he was with one crew, the other would concentrate on illustrating his words.

Filming was to start off in Easter Island, so once more I found myself on the Jumbo to Santiago in Chile, and then the weekly DC3 to Easter Island.

There were no hotels on the island and the six of us were accommodated in various private houses. Producer Dick Gilling and I were staying with a couple called Rosa and Cardinali who made us very welcome. They possessed a rather cheeky parrot called Pedro, and the bird and I quickly made friends. If I held a pencil aloft he would hang upside down from it and look at me in a very mischievous way whilst telling jokes in Spanish. If this bird had turned professional he would have had a great career in stand-up or rather hang-down.

While we waited for Doctor Bronowski to arrive we did some time-lapse photography on the huge statues for which the island is famous. My assistant David Swann and myself set up a camera on a sturdy support to include a group of seven of these identical stone giants, looking at the sky with their empty eye sockets and uncomprehending faces.

The reason for time-lapse was that I wanted to compress a complete day from sunrise to sunset into about 30 seconds so that the shadows of the statues cast by the sun would continuously move in the changing light. For normal TV cinematography, the camera takes twenty-five pictures per second. I calculated that if the camera were to take only one picture every minute, this would condense the day into the 30 or so seconds we needed. We had a timer that could take one frame every 60 seconds automatically. To make the shot more interesting, I wanted the camera to zoom in slowly over the 30 seconds until the shot finishes with a big close-up of the face of one of the statues. This would mean in practice, that the zoom would have to take about twelve hours in real time. There are now complex electronic devices that will do this, and you can see these at work in nature films showing plants growing etc. However this was an unplanned idea so I achieved this effect with a bucket and a wooden block! A tiny hole was made near the bottom of the bucket, which was filled, with water. A wooden block was floated on top of the water and a piece of string attached to the block. The other end of the string was wound round the zoom control of the lens As the water level almost imperceptibly went down, the string gradually moved the zoom lens until it reached its closest position. Very Heath Robinson, but it worked. There was no crime on the island and we were able to leave the camera to take its pictures and

Filming for *The Ascent of Man* in Arizona 1971 with Simon Wilson (left) and Rick Stratton (centre)

do other things, returning every so often to make sure that everything was working correctly.

Two days later Doctor Bronowski arrived. He was staying with Dick and myself at Rosa and Cardinali's house. *The Ascent of Man* was an expensive production by television standards and the BBC had insured Bronowski for several million pounds. This had involved a very thorough medical examination and that and the long flight meant that he had arrived in an exhausted state and with a terrible cold. This was not a good start.

I always carried with me some Olbas oil, which is a volatile and extremely powerful medication for the relief of bronchial and nasal congestion. It has a very strong smell, but it works. I gave this to the Doctor and he took it up to bed with him.

The next morning at breakfast he seemed much improved. How is your cold?' I enquired. He looked at me, quite irritated. 'My cold is much better but I have had to throw away my pyjama,' he retorted, in the voice I remembered so fondly from his Brains Trust days.

Actually the more I saw of the Doctor the more I liked him. In stature he was diminutive but dynamically shaped. His enthusiasm shone through, and if there were a point you didn't understand, he would explain it as painstakingly as if he were addressing millions of viewers. He dressed smartly and always wore very expensive hand-made shoes. This, I was told, was the direct result of often being barefoot as a child, coming as he did, from a poor family in Poland.

The three-month trip continued. It took us to Chile, Guatemala, Peru, Honduras, Brazil and the USA. The Doctor would arrive to appear before the camera in each country. He worked entirely without a script, and would usually get it right in three takes. The first take was always too long; the second better and third perfect. If it were necessary to go beyond the third take, his performance would invariably tail off. He was not a young man and all that travel is quite exhausting.

After three months we returned home for some brief leave; then the shooting continued, filming extensively across Europe and in Britain.

On the 25th November we arrived in Afghanistan and travelled to Mazar-e-Sharif to film the *buzkashi*, a violent wargame said to have been invented by Genghis Khan. The participants ride specially-bred fiery horses. There are many riders taking part but it is not a team game, but a game to decide a champion. It is played not with a ball but with the carcase of a calf weighing about 50 lbs. and the object is for a player to snatch it up from the centre of a large field, defending it against all challengers, and carrying it off through two stages. The first stage of the game is riding with the carcase to the fixed boundary flag and rounding the flag. After that the crucial stage is the return. As he sweeps round the flag, constantly challenged, the rider heads for home and the goal, which is a marked circle in which he has to deposit the carcase. The game is going to be won by a single goal, so no quarter is given. There is nothing in the rules about fair play. The tactics are pure Mongol and riders and horses are very aggressive.

To film this exciting spectacle I used a 600 mm lens on one camera and shot some of it with a special slow-motion camera. The game was eventually over and the victorious but battered champion had been declared. I needed some extra shots that would have been impossible to get at the time, so we mounted the camera on an open Citroen 2CV. These cars were initially designed for French farmers to use in their fields; the suspension can smooth out violent bumps and they are excellent for taking moving shots over rough ground. I asked, through our interpreter, for about dozen mounted riders to 'chase' the camera as we hurtled over the rough ground. This didn't quite turn out as planned. The horses were much faster than the vehicle and a galloping, snarling horse, a few inches away from my lens, tried to bite off my right ear. But it was all great fun and I got some good shots. Give a cameraman a bit of pure action and he is happy.

The next day was a rest day. Days off on location are always a bit of a problem. It is quite difficult to unwind after an action-packed week and we would often wander around rather aimlessly. There are also domestic matters to attend to like getting laundry done. Since the hotel facilities were somewhat unpredictable I decided to do this myself, and was contemplating the rather sad sight of a bath full of socks, shirts and underpants floating in soapsuds, when there was a knock on the door of my room. It was our two Afghan helpers. They were going duck-shooting and wanted to know if any of us would like to come along. In the end executive producer Adrian Malone, assistant director David Kennard and myself opted to accompany them. The rest of the crew decided to do their own thing.

We drove for over an hour, eventually coming to a wide river and parked on the bank. One of our guides grinned and pointed to the other side of the river.

'Russia,' he said. Adrian looked surprised.

'Surely we are not allowed to shoot here.' The Afghan shrugged.

'No problem,' he said, 'we come here all the time'.

Our two guides supervised the loading of our guns and we raised them and took pot shots at the Afghan (or were they Russian?) ducks. After half an hour or so the ducks had all skilfully managed to avoid our bullets and I was following one of them through my rifle sights, trying to muster my panning skills, when I saw an open jeep in the distance speeding towards us. It skidded to a halt in a cloud of dust and two Afghan policemen got out and started shouting at our two guides. In the back of the jeep sat a grim-faced Russian who remained silent. After our guides had tried to explain what we were doing there we were escorted back to Mazar-e-Sharif police station and searched. As luck would have it David Kennard had his Minnox camera in his pocket, which he had bought at a duty free airport shop somewhere on our travels. The Minnox is marvel of miniaturised engineering being only a few inches long. It had a reputation for being used as a spy camera and indeed it is designed to copy documents easily. The Russian looked even more grim-faced. This was at the height of the 'cold war' and the part of the Russian border where we were shooting, was the area that was used for rocket and space research - highly secret. We were kept at the police station for several hours while our poor guides were grilled endlessly. Then the Russian, who it transpired spoke good English, interrogated us. After the Minnox film had been found to contain only pictures of the *buzkashi* and members of the unit grinning inanely, much to our relief we were finally released and drove back to our hotel where we explained what had happened to the others. I think that they were disappointed that they had not been with us to share the adventure. A few beers later I returned wearily to my room. There was my washing still floating in the bath, a sight I could have done without.

On 27th January 1972 I travelled to Doctor Bronowski's home in La Jolla, California, for programme 13. This final programme in the series depicted the Doctor wandering around his house talking to the camera and summing up the previous programmes. I filmed this by being propelled around in a wheelchair being used as an improvised dolly. We could have used all the trappings of Hollywood, grips dollies etc., but since this was an intensely personal and emotional contribution from Bronowski, the number of people in the house was kept to a minimum.

After the lengthy editing process the films were finally ready for transmission. Every one who had worked on the series was invited to the Television Centre in White City to have tea with the Doctor and his wife. We were presented with a signed copy of his book of the series, *The Ascent of Man.*

The programmes were transmitted, to much acclaim. Doctor Bronowski died a year later in 1974.

English Landscapes

In 1976 and 1977, I worked on a series of 12 illustrated essays on the English Landscape. The series of films was entitled *One Man's England* and was written and presented by Professor W. G. Hoskins, described in the *Times Educational Supplement* as 'the most gifted interpreter of the English Landscape any of us are likely to see.' The programme titles were, Ancient Dorset, The Lake District: The Conquest of the Mountains, North Norfolk: Marsh and Sea, Kent: Landscapes of War and Peace, The Black Country, The Deserted Midlands, Cornwall: Behind the Scenery, Leicestershire: The Fox and the Covert, Derbyshire: No Stone Unturned, Norfolk and Suffolk: Breckland and Broads, Northumberland: The Making of a Frontier and Devon: Land of my Fathers.

The producer was Peter Jones, who had worked on Horizon programmes and was involved in many Natural History films. Sound was recorded by Simon Wilson, and my assistants over the two year period were Mike Radford, Neil Kennedy and Rick Stratton. In the list of acknowledgements in Hoskins' book of the series, *One Man's England*, he writes, 'The Producer's assistants, Sheila Johns and Rita Cooper, made all the practical side work smoothly though one of them refused an order to lay her head on the rails of the main London-Edinburgh line to tell us if she could hear a train coming for the cameraman's benefit.'

Photographing landscapes may seem like a fairly simple task but I felt that there was a danger of making the images too romantic. The films were about how man has influenced the landscape and romance was not part of my brief. I decided that I would shoot in any conditions that came our way, and not wait for the light to be ideal. Thus we shot in blizzards, downpours, howling gales and foggy mornings; in fact anything that the weather could throw at us. I have to say that it was a most delightful series to work on. Bill Hoskins liked to have his wine at lunchtime and in the afternoon his face would become bright red. There were worried calls from the film laboratory about his changing colour, so I made sure that all his pieces to camera were shot in the morning.

In each programme there were quite a lot of helicopter shots since these could show certain aspects of the landscape, more clearly than from ground level. My pilot was Tim Wheeldon who was brilliant at placing the helicopter virtually anywhere in the sky. Each programme involved a day in the Jet Ranger for Peter Jones and myself, flying and circling to get the pictures we needed. Tim had removed the door and I sat on the floor with my legs sticking out and resting on the skids. It was a strange experience when the helicopter tilted me towards the ground with nothing between eternity and me although of course I was well strapped in place. On one occasion we were skimming over a small forest. 'Can you get a bit lower, Tim?' I asked though my intercom.

'Coming up,' said Tim. I took the shot.

'That was good, Tim. Can you get just a bit closer to the treetops?'

Tim went lower still and I was finally happy with the shot. When we landed, I found that there were small twigs with leaves stuck in my shoes. I guess that was about as low as Tim could get.

For the Lake District filming I had my dog Kip with me and at lunchtimes he accompanied us to a pub in Keswick. The professor had firmly stated that he had no affinity with dogs whatsoever and told me some anti-dog stories to prove it. One lunchtime, as we were getting ready to go back to work I called Kip who was in his usual place under our table. Uncharacteristically he refused to come out. Then I remembered that I had forgotten to order his piece of cheese from the bar, which had become a daily ritual. Once Kip had been given this, he followed me, tail wagging. The professor was very impressed with this, being something of a trencherman himself, and I noticed that when he thought that I wasn't looking he would pat Kip on the head.

Some time after filming had been completed, sadly Kip died and when a copy of the professor's book was presented to me he had written on the flyleaf, 'For Nat in memory of old Kip who hung around for his cheese – Bill.'

Some time later I acquired another bull terrier, Smudge, who took on the role of the cameraman's dog. He loved film people but he became infamous for eating his way out of hotel rooms and film generator vans to see where I was.

Professor Bill Hoskins with my dog, Smudge

The Spongers

On the 22nd August 1977 I started work on a Play for Today, entitled *The Spongers*. The Producer and Director were the highly respected Tony Garnett and Roland Joffe.

The Spongers is a grim and gritty piece written by Jim Allan, and is based on a true story about a mother unable to cope on her own with three children including one with Downs Syndrome. She is unable to navigate the well-meaning but confusing maze of bureaucracy set up to help by the Labour government of the period, and it all ends in horrifying tragedy.

Before shooting began, the actress playing the mother and the three children all previously unknown to each other, lived together for three weeks as a family in the main location, a Middleton housing estate in the North of England.

Roland brought further realism to the project by getting the actors to improvise the dialogue within scenes. Usually film drama is highly structured. The actors move to predetermined marks placed on the floor, perhaps to catch a light or to form dynamic groupings with other actors. They learn the dialogue more or less word for word; indeed in a Dennis Potter script the author did not allow one syllable to be changed. This is a part of the film actor's craft and some are better than others at allocating part of their mind to the mechanics of film-making, while submerging themselves in the character they are playing. Joffe did not want the actors to be distracted in any way. He wanted them to be completely unaware of the camera and to play their scenes as if it didn't exist and for them to improvise the scenes within the structure of the script. This produced a raw documentary effect and it gave me some interesting challenges. For instance there is one scene where a councillor and two bailiffs, enter the debt-ridden mother's house to remove her furniture. I was in a corner of the room with the camera. On cue five people burst into the room and performed the scene totally without regard to the camera's position. I grabbed what I could of the mêlée. The scene was done several times, each time differently, and each time I shot close-ups of different actors. When all the material was edited together, the scene was very realistic and not at all like actors acting.

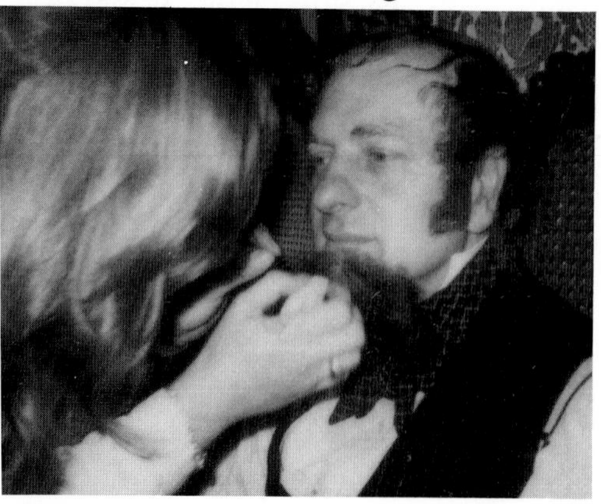

When filming *Tis Pity she's a Whore* with Roland Joffe he persuaded me to play a wedding photographer, a part for which someone had forgotten to order an actor.

Roland Joffe is a very cool director. I never once heard him raise his voice or have a tantrum, as some of the more flamboyant directors seem to enjoy doing. He created an extraordinary atmosphere both for the actors and the unit. After filming the tense scenes there was always a respectful silence. I don't think I have ever seen a hard-bitten film unit so affected by the work they were involved in. *The Spongers* was awarded a Prix Italia.

Blue Remembered Hills

I consider myself very lucky to have been given such interesting dramas to photograph. In August 1978 I was to shoot the film, *Blue Remembered Hills,* written by Dennis Potter, produced by Ken Trodd and directed by Brian Gibson.

The location is the forest of Dean, where Potter had spent his childhood. The action takes place during the Second World War and depicts the adventures of seven young children playing in the forest.

Colin Welland, Helen Mirren, John Bird, Janine Duvitsky, Robin Ellis, Michael Elphick, and Colin Jeavons played the seven-year-old children. It says something for their work and that of director Gibson, that when viewing the film, after the initial shock, the audience accepted that it was watching children.

Colin Welland told me how difficult it was to play a seven-year-old, because he had to force his mature body to gyrate and cavort as children do. Because the actors were seldom still, using the convention of long shots, mid shots and close-ups didn't seem to work. Instead we shot the scenes as a series of choreographed tableaux, the actor's violent movements contained within a static frame. The forest too creates its own atmosphere, and I was very pleased when Colin Welland said after a viewing, that the forest was like another character. Some of the scenes take place in a barn and the props department built a wooden ladder and other props scaled up to twice their normal size to make the actors look smaller. In the forest exteriors, there were huge trees to further dwarf them. We· were blessed with abundant sunshine during the filming which helped to reinforce the child-like images that Brian and I were trying to create.

Going Gently

Director Stephen Frears and I have worked on three films together. The first, *Long Distance Information,* was about an Elvis Presley afficionado who presents a music programme on a local English radio station. He is away from his microphone embroiled in an icy dinner party with his ex-wife and current girl friend, when news of Presley's death is announced. When he finally gets to hear the news he is devastated and hurries to the radio station to broadcast a eulogy to his mourning listeners. Elvis's haunting music is played throughout.

I particularly liked working with Stephen. He is a cameraman's director and inspired me to produce exciting crane shots and dramatic lighting. This is something I enjoy doing when the subject calls for it, although on most films restraint is necessary to keep the camerawork unobtrusive.

June 9th, 1980. The second Stephen Frears film, *Going Gently,* produced by Innes Lloyd, is a hospital drama. When I read the script I became a bit depressed. It is about two elderly men dying in a cancer ward. I couldn't see how this could make an entertaining film. I hadn't reckoned on Innes and Stephen's casting. Norman Wisdom and Fulton Mckay played the patients.

Left: Is the sun going to be out for long enough? Helen Mirren in the background

Janine Duvitsky, Michael Elphick, John Bird, Helen Mirren, Colin Welland, and Robin Ellis in Blue Remembered Hills by Dennis Potter

Right: Brian Gibson and N.C.with Helen Mirren and Janine Duvitsky

Stephen asked me how I was going to photograph the play. I suggested that the images should work against the bleakness of the subject. Almost all of the action takes place in a hospital ward and it seemed to me that the lighting should be constantly changing: sunsets, sunrises, thunderstorms at night and golden afternoons. The camera should be restless, hurtling through the corridors, hovering over the beds, exploring the hospital architecture. The location of the film is a disused hospital in Ealing.

I had always been a fan of Norman Wisdom's work and meeting him in the flesh was no disappointment. True to form, he would say to Stephen,

'Shall I fall out of bed at this point?'

'No Norman, do nothing, just lie there,' was Stephen's direction.

Throughout the filming Stephen was heard constantly saying, 'Do nothing, Norman.' Norman was of course playing a serious role, though not without its comic overtones, and he gave a very moving performance. One scene required him to be lighting a cigar. We did the scene several times and each time, knowing that I was a cigar-smoker, he passed them with exaggerated secrecy to me. He and Fulton seem to be a perfect match and Judi Dench gave a brilliantly restrained performance as the ward sister. In spite of my initial doubts it proved to be a very jolly film to work on. Stephen received a BAFTA award for his direction, and so did I for the photography.

The third film was *Song of Experience,* a story of three young train-spotters in the 60s, a tale of sexual discovery and lost innocence. As well as images of some wonderful old steam locomotives, the film contained quite a lot of explicit dialogue and strong language. Innes, who produced, thought that some of it was gratuitous and might upset some viewers who thought that they would be watching a different kind of film. Stephen refused to cut any of it, feeling that the language was essential to the piece. Naturally directors are fiercely protective of their work, but the producer has the last word and there was at one stage the possibility that the film would not be transmitted. Eventually some minor cuts were made and the film went out, but as far as I know was never repeated. It's a shame; I thought it was a good film.

A Portrait

On 1st February 1981 I received a letter from John Bratby, the artist, stating that he would like to paint my portrait. I immediately thought that this was a practical joke perpetrated by one of my colleagues. I suspected fellow-cameraman John Wyatt who was well known for his impish sense of humour. But no, this turned out to be genuine. I was puzzled to know why he had selected me. I can only guess that he had seen a film that I had photographed on the life of Paul Gauguin for Monitor.

A few days later I travelled to the Cupola and Tower of the Winds, Belmont Road, Hastings. I was greeted by Mr Bratby who led the way up a staircase to his studio. I decided not to ask why he had chosen me in case it was a matter of mistaken identity! He required me to sit for four hours and promised that during the session his wife would serve the best bacon sandwiches that I have ever tasted. She did and they were. At the end of the session, during which he talked to me continuously, the painting was finished and he looked exhausted.

Eventually, after it had appeared in an exhibition, I purchased his painting and it hangs in my house. John Bratby has also painted the Queen Mother and Paul McCartney so I am very flattered that he chose me.

Ruby in the Rain

March 2nd, 1981. Depart for Belfast to film a Play for Today, *Iris in the Traffic, Ruby in the Rain*. I didn't find working in Belfast quite as harrowing as I had expected. As usual the peaceful moments are never reported. We were filming in a derelict house and during the lunch break I stayed behind for a while to read the script. When I finally made my way to the catering wagon, parked a few streets away, I saw three soldiers with their guns trained on the members of the unit who, completely unaware of this, were contentedly munching on their jam roly poly and custard. The soldiers then realised who they were and quietly disappeared. Quite surreal.

On another occasion I was having supper at Cheerios, a restaurant that several local people had recommended. There was a very large fellow at the next table who looked a bit like Orson Wells. We struck up a conversation. He was a surgeon at the local hospital and also spent a large part of his time travelling the world lecturing on the treatment of bullet wounds, on which he was a leading authority.

A Soldier's Tale

July 20th, 1981. Peter Adam was well known for making documentaries for the Music and Arts Department Some time previously he had produced Stravinsky's *A Soldier's Tale* for a concert at the Festival Hall. He was now to recreate this for television. I was delighted that I was asked to do it, as I like this piece. I was a little troubled by the fact that we only had four days to shoot what I thought was quite a complex project. We were to shoot at Riverside Studios where an enormous set had been built depicting the village, and the devil's house. I had a day to pre-light with six electricians and my lighting gaffer, Tommy Moran. The scenes take place at various times of day and night and often the light changes had to occur in vision, as in a theatre. We had a huge bank of dimmers and by the time we had completed the lighting set-up, there were enough cables behind the set to knit a battleship.

The next day we began filming. Wayne Sleep played the soldier and Ben Kingsley, the narrator. We shot in sequence; thus Ben Kingsley began the piece.

Down a hot and dusty road,
Tramps a soldier with his load
Ten days' leave he has to spend
Will his journey never end?
Marching home, marching on his way
Marching, marching all the day
Soon he will be home to stay,
He's been marching all the day,
Happy now he's home to stay.

I had two cameras covering the action so that to save time, we could do long takes in close-up and wide shots simultaneously. I do not think that the director had tackled anything on quite this scale before. I was always ready if help was needed, but he had developed a rapport with my young assistant. Any suggestions by him were treated with rapturous approval. My input was received with a certain amount of disdain. Being under pressure can affect directors in different ways. In one scene Wayne Sleep has to pull his violin out of a knapsack. It momentarily got stuck and Wayne let out a little 'eek' of mock alarm. We all laughed and prepared for take two, but Peter Adam, not particularly well known for his placid nature, screamed at Wayne across the crowded studio floor and gave him a public roasting at the top of his voice. Wayne, astonished by this outburst and feeling that he had been unfairly humiliated, started to walk out. Adam screamed at him to get back on the set. Wayne, professional as he is, did as he was bid.

We finished the project on time, but I felt it was under-shot and didn't have any particular style, and I think Adam realised that producing the piece for television was very different from producing for the concert hall. However the breakfasts at the little transport café opposite the studio, were excellent.

With Barry Davies shooting *The Year of a Child* in Dublin

Cruel Garden

I had photographed several ballet films with director Colin Nears. I always enjoyed photographing these as I liked their theatricality (probably originating from my childhood visits to the Ilford Hippodrome). For once, I didn't have to be too concerned with naturalistic lighting. It could be over the top and dramatic.

I usually did my own operating and I found it was quite challenging to follow dancers, panning and tilting the camera as they leapt around the stage. As Colin had taught me, not one fingertip or toe must be lost out of frame, yet you had to be brave enough not to make the shot too wide. A bit like filming a football match I suppose.

On the 30th July 1981 we started work on the Ballet Rambert's production of *Cruel Garden.* This is a strong piece of ballet-drama about the life of the poet, Federico Garcia Lorca. The choreographer and lead dancer was Christopher Bruce. We were to shoot the production in Studio 3A at Ealing, using the ballet company's touring sets which were to be erected by the rigging crew the night before we began shooting. The lighting was complex with many light changes cued to the action. In the theatre, computerised lighting desks are permanently installed, and the various lighting set-ups are pre-set and put into computer memory. The operators of these desks become very proficient as they use them on a daily basis. Ealing is an old film studio and its own lighting system, while being perfectly adequate for drama filming could not cope with the complexities of lighting for ballet. This meant that a lighting desk had to be hired in for a particular production, and due to some union agreement in force at the time, had to be operated by in-house electricians. Of course it was ridiculous to expect a film electrician suddenly to have to cope with a whole new technology when an expert from the theatre was standing by doing nothing, but that's the way it was.

The set couldn't be erected until the last minute, due to other productions using the studio space. This meant that I had to design the lighting plot, working from a drawing of the set. I completed this in good time and was quite pleased with the way it had come together. My gaffer and his electricians were able to set all the lights on the overhead lighting rail from my plan, and it would only be necessary to give the lights a final tweak, once the set was in place. The hired lighting desk too had been installed and we were lucky enough to have it operated by a bright spark who, after some practice, was fairly confident.

On the morning we were to start shooting I arrived at the studio and looked at the set. I froze in my tracks. The huge set was amazing. It was a bullring, but ingeniously could be turned into many other things. But the reason for my freezure was that because the set had been built for the theatre it was much higher than our standard studio sets. In fact it was so high it almost touched the lighting rails where we had spent the previous day carefully setting the lights. It meant that my lighting rig was useless, the set would block half the lights. No one had foreseen this, least of all me. The dancers were already there limbering up, and a little bead of sweat rolled down my cheek.

My lighting crew were brilliant. Within an hour I had completely re-lit from scratch using mainly floor lighting. It may not have looked quite as good as the lighting I had planned, but I think that I got away with it. The film was awarded a Prix Italia.

Country

James Fox and Wendy Hiller

In 1945 the brewing giants, the Carlions, assemble at a large country house for a family gathering. The war has just ended and the present head of the business, Sir Frederick, is getting old and the decision of who will take over the Empire must be made. One of the younger members of the family produces a sample of a new kind of beer that has a much longer storage life and will be more profitable. Sir Frederick takes a sip and spits it out in disgust. 'Gnat's piss' is his reaction. Nevertheless they decide to go ahead with the production of keg beer.

Country was written by Trevor Griffiths, directed by Richard Eyre and produced by Ann Scott. We began filming in autumn 1980.

Richard confided that he was feeling a bit nervous of directing the very powerful cast that had been assembled. Frederick Alexander, Jill Bennett, James Fox, Joan Greenwood, Wendy Hiller, Leo McKern and Frederick Treves. I do not think that Sir Richard Eyre would have that problem today. What a pity that people have to grow up!

Ballroom of Romance

We are in County Mayo in Southern Ireland. The Ballroom of Romance is an old wooden hut in the middle of nowhere. Every Saturday night its sign lights up and the glittering ball of mirrors in its stark interior, slowly revolves. It fills with young men and women from the isolated farms in the county. The men stand on one side of the hall, the women on the other. Every so often a man will approach and ask a girl to dance to the music of the four-man Romantic Orchestra.

Bridie, who lives on a small farm with her disabled father, is no longer young and she has been going to the Ballroom of Romance for a long time. She is in love with the drummer of the Romantic Orchestra but he does not seem interested in her. She decides that perhaps this will be her last visit. As the evening ends one of the regulars, who has been after Bridie for some time and is a bit worse for drink as usual, approaches her. He is nothing like the drummer but she resignedly accepts his proposal of marriage and goes off with him to the fields.

The script was written from a William Trevor short story. Ken Trodd produced, Pat O'Connor directed, and Brenda Flicker played Bridie with a splendid cast of Irish actors. We started filming in September/October 1981.

Since the location was the lovely Achill Island in County Mayo, it seemed like a good idea to rent a cottage for the duration of filming. Anne and Smudge the dog flew over with me, and my assistant John Beck stayed at the cottage with us. Every morning he and I set out for the one-hour dappled drive to the location, the ramshackle shack in the middle of nowhere. I had pre-lit the 'ballroom' and since most of the action took place within the shack it was usually only necessary to switch on the lights, make small adjustments and we were ready to film. I was operating as well, so I had plenty to keep me occupied.

The filming progressed well as we worked through William Trevor's delightful story. The owners of our cottage in Achill appeared at the door on two or three occasions with a pair of live lobsters and a huge circle of soda bread. John Beck, a huntin' and fishin' man, made short work of cooking the lobsters and I must say they were delicious. At the end of the day's work there were walks and pleasant evenings in the friendly local hostelry.

At the completion of filming we had our end-of-shoot party in the large crumbling house where the director and production personnel were staying. Pat O'Connor got slightly smashed and was quite emotional as he lavishly praised everybody in the unit.

Quite often it seemed that if you'd had a good time on location the film could turn out to be slightly disappointing and vice versa. This time it was excellent on both counts.

A Drink with Oliver Reed

In December 1981 there was a series called *Jobs for the Boys*. The presenter, whose name I can't remember, was given a different job to do in each programme and before each one he was briefed by an expert. In this instance he was to appear as a small-time crook in a feature film, and to help him achieve his tough-guy image, he was to be briefed on camera by Oliver Reed.

We arrived at Oliver Reed's farm in Sussex at about 9 a.m. Oliver was yet to make an appearance so we began setting up the camera and lights in the living room. There were three builders there who were very helpful and I had the feeling that they had been engaged to do some building work but somehow had never gone away.

Eventually Oliver appeared in black leather calf-length boots, smouldering as only he could. He was pleased to see me and we had a brief chat about the Ken Russell film that we had both worked on. The filming started and Oliver was very amusing on camera with his advice to the wimpish presenter.

Although only one eye is used to look through the camera viewfinder I usually keep both eyes open. The 'spare' eye can often spot something outside the current frame, which might be used as the next shot. This is particularly useful when filming for a documentary. During Oliver's interview my left eye was firmly glued to the viewfinder and my right eye was roving around as usual when it spotted a strange bright object slowly advancing towards me. I couldn't quite make out what it was. It was shiny and was making a tinkling noise. My vision cleared and I saw that the object was a huge vodka and tonic being handed to me by one of the builders. It was only 10.30 a.m. but not wishing to appear standoffish, I accepted the glass. All this was happening whilst we were in the middle of shooting. We completed the sequence about an hour later and I was pleased that I had the rest of the day to organise the next day's work. As we were wrapping the gear and loading the car, the producer hurried up to me. 'I've just found out it's Oliver's birthday,' he said excitedly. 'I'm just popping down to the village for some champagne, would you mind hanging on?' I nodded. When the producer returned, Oliver and his cronies joined us and we toasted his birthday. I started saying my goodbyes.

'Have you got a minute?' smiled Oliver. 'I'll take you on a short tour.' I nodded. He led the way to a large barn. 'This is where we make our cider; I have several different varieties, try this one.' After trying three different varieties we left the barn and moved on to another building in his garden. 'This is the pub,' he said. 'I'm barred from the village pub so I had to build my own.'

Suddenly the presence of the builders made sense. Having built the pub it would obviously need to have routine maintenance. What could be more efficient than keeping a permanent staff for this purpose? The interior of the pub was authentic in every detail and Oliver demonstrated how perfectly beer could be poured. I nodded. Things started to become a bit hazy at that point. I do remember later that evening that there was a group led by Oliver, lustily singing sea shanties round the piano and that I was the accompanist. This was puzzling because without any false modesty, I can claim that my piano playing is pretty appalling. I am not quite sure when the evening ended but I think it was well after midnight. Everyone in the small unit appeared to have had a good time, particularly Pat the director who, as a farewell gesture, performed a moving rendition of 'When Irish eyes are smiling'.

This was meant to have been a quick morning shoot. I am not sure that I could have survived a three-week documentary.

Casper Weinberger

December 10th, 1981. Casper Weinberger the US defence secretary was making a lightning trip to London and we were waiting at a Portman Square hotel to interview him for Nationwide. Of course as a cameraman I was quite rightly not expected to make any kind of political comment, but no one seemed to realise that photography can be a comment. Mr Weinberger arrived with a group of hard-faced staff. I thought him a bit creepy and rather sinister, and I think my lighting may have instinctively reflected this. Let's just say that it was rather different from the lighting I had used for Mother Theresa when we interviewed her in India. Mr Weinberger was subsequently charged with involvement with the Iran-Contra affair. President Bush later pardoned him.

Bell-jar Meringues

In my spare time I enjoy cooking, I find it relaxing. I was interested to meet an Oxford don (sorry, I've forgotten his name) who used science to cook and gave jokey lectures on his technique. We travelled to Oxford to film in his lab. His first dish was Inverted Baked Alaska. I am sure that you know that normal baked Alaska consists of a frozen block of ice cream surrounded by a blanket of meringue. It is put into a hot oven for a short period, the meringue cooks but the ice-cream, protected by the meringue, stays hard. His idea was to reverse this and have a central core of hot meringue and jam surrounded by ice cream. To achieve this he used a microwave oven that cooks from the centre outwards. Result: the centre hot, the outer ice cream hard, the teeth painful.

His next experiment was to cook meringues in a vacuum jar. They expanded to enormous proportions, but it was like eating a cloud.

Dinner at his house was a relaxed affair. The roast pork had a temperature probe inserted, which was connected to a graph read-out machine in the dining room. He could sit drinking wine with his guests until the exact temperature of the meat was reached. Before roasting he had, by means of a hypodermic syringe, injected the pork with fresh pineapple juice, an enzyme, which has high tenderising properties. One of the guests was Michel Roux and when asked what was his opinion of the meat said that he thought it was an interesting way of making pineapple-flavoured paté!

Intensive Care

May 2nd, 1982. Work begins on Alan Bennet's, *Intensive Care* with Alan and Julie Walters, directed by Gavin Millar, produced by Innes Lloyd.

Finish filming in Leeds 28th May and get home to find that Anne's 15-year holiday is over. She is about to return to New Zealand, unable to accept my constant travelling and the rift that seems to have developed between us. I'm saddened, but make no attempt to persuade her otherwise. It means that there is no one to look after Smudge, the dog, when I am abroad. Regretfully he has to go into a kennel during my trip to Cuba. I decided that the best place to take him would be to the breeder he originally came from in Poole, Dorset, since he would know her.

Alicia Alonso

June 18th, 1982. Took the early morning flight from Madrid to Havana in a Cuban Airways Russian Jet. The plane was full mostly with Cubans who had been holidaying in Spain and were returning with souvenirs of the trip. The flight was timed to leave before sun-up while the temperature was still cool. Later, the summer heat would have made the take-off more difficult because the plane was heavy with fuel and passengers for the long flight. Most of the passengers had bought portable stereos in Madrid and as soon as the plane was airborne they proudly started to play them, all with different tapes, a cacophony of noise.

I was travelling to Cuba with a small documentary unit to make a film about Alicia Alonso, the ballerina and choreographer.

The next day, after what seemed like an eternity, we landed at Havana.

We had Sunday off to recover and on the 21st we started filming with the Cuban National Ballet.

Alicia Alonso was born in 1921. She danced on Broadway before soloing with several companies. She created her Cuban Ballet Company in 1948, now known as the National Ballet. We were privileged to watch and film her dance *Giselle*, in spite of her then being 61.

One night, as a treat, our interpreter took us to the Tropicana, an outdoor nightclub. It was tacky and kitsch and quite magnificent. The show was on such a vast scale that the curtains were made of steam! There seemed to be hundreds of dancers and the whole thing reminded me of the Hollywood musicals of my youth. We finished up by drinking daiquiris in Hemingway's bar. You see it's not all suffering.

At the Monte Christo cigar factory we watched about fifty men and women sitting at tables, hand-rolling these most expensive luxuries so coveted by the capitalist world. The atmosphere seemed very peaceful and the only sounds were the soothing voice of a storyteller and the gentle crackling of tobacco leaves.

At the end of the Cuban trip, I arrived at London Airport at about 10 p. m. and a car was waiting to take me home to Surrey. It seemed strange coming back to the empty house without Anne or Smudge. I phoned the kennel to find out how Smudge was doing. The young son answered. 'He's OK,' he said, 'but he's been crying a lot.'

'I am coming down there now to pick him up,' I said. It was a two-hour drive to Dorset, but Smudge and I were both pleased to see each other.

An Englishman Abroad

In October 1982 Innes Lloyd called me to a meeting with John Schlesinger. This was not the first time that I had met him. Way back in 1961 I had worked on a one-day story in Petticoat Lane, London, for Tonight and John was the director. But now he had gone on to do great things, including directing one of my favourite films, *Midnight Cowboy*. I was to photograph a film drama entitled *An Englishman Abroad.* Written by Alan Bennett the play was based on a true story of a meeting between defector Guy Burgess and actress Coral Browne in Moscow, while she was on tour in *Hamlet* with the Shakespeare Memorial Company. In our film Coral Browne was playing herself and Alan Bates was to play Guy Burgess.

The play was set in Moscow but relations between Russia and the West were then not good enough for the Russians to allow filming to take place in Moscow, particularly in view of the subject matter. (Apart from which our budget would not have stretched to it.) It was decided that Glasgow and Dundee were to represent the exteriors of Moscow. I attended two days of rehearsals at the BBC rehearsal rooms in Goldhawk Road, where I met Coral Browne and Alan Bates. Coral Browne was a brash and likeable Australian actress who was then in her seventies. The make-up Department and I had to make her look fiftyish, as she was when the incident in Moscow had occurred.

With John Schlesinger filming *An Englishman Abroad*

On 30th January 1983 the camera, sound and lighting crews set out from Ealing for Glasgow and the next day we started shooting. The first scene we did was in fact the very ending of the film, Alan Bates strolling across the Suspension Bridge in Glasgow in his new clothes. As we began filming, with designer Stuart Walker's huge posters of Stalin making the scene look very Russian, a blizzard began, with driving snow almost blotting out the landscape. Actually this was a bonus and made the scene look even more convincing. The scenes on the vast staircase outside the British Embassy were shot in Glasgow Town Hall, an extraordinary building well worth a visit for anyone in the vicinity. The interior of the Embassy was filmed in Polesden Lacey in Surrey. The exterior of the theatre and the street scenes with Coral looking for Guy Burgess's flat were shot in Dundee. As real snow had been established it was necessary to keep this going although the budget had not allowed for that. Stuart did a deal with the Dundee Borough Council, and tons of road salt was laid on the roads and pavements where we were shooting. It looked very much like the real thing. The interior of Guy's flat was a set built in Caird Hall, Dundee, so we were able sometimes to shoot exteriors during the day and interiors in the evening. The shooting was completed in three weeks, something of a record I believe.

During the filming Alan Bennett was there every day, all day, watching anxiously over the interpretation of his script. At one point he felt that something was not quite right and made a discreet comment to the director. 'There is only one good author,' exploded Schlesinger, 'and that's a dead one.' Bennett looked hurt. Actually in Hollywood at this time, and probably even now, writers were not allowed near the set. In fact security men were employed to make sure they didn't sneak in to see the actors performing their lines. BBC Television is altogether more civilised, although the money is not as good.

The film opens with Guy Burgess in a packed theatre in Moscow, watching the performance of *Hamlet*. We filmed this in a theatre in Dundee. We had about forty extras, and I had to make it look as if the auditorium was full.

I carefully arranged the extras in the theatre seats and framed very tightly so that I was cutting off just before the empty seats. After the shooting had been completed, John Schlesinger and I saw the remainder of the rushes at Ealing. When this scene came up, I saw that the camera was actually shooting slightly more than I had seen in the viewfinder, and empty seats could be seen. 'Oh disaster!' cried John. 'Absolute disaster.' I was hoping the floor of the viewing room would open and swallow me up.

The film editor, Ken Pearce, came to the rescue. 'No problem,' he calmly said, 'I'll get the labs to slightly blow up the picture.'

An Englishman Abroad received several BAFTAs including one for my work. The then Prime Minister, Margaret Thatcher, requested a copy to view during the Christmas parliamentary recess. It has been repeated several times and I feel fortunate to have been associated with it.

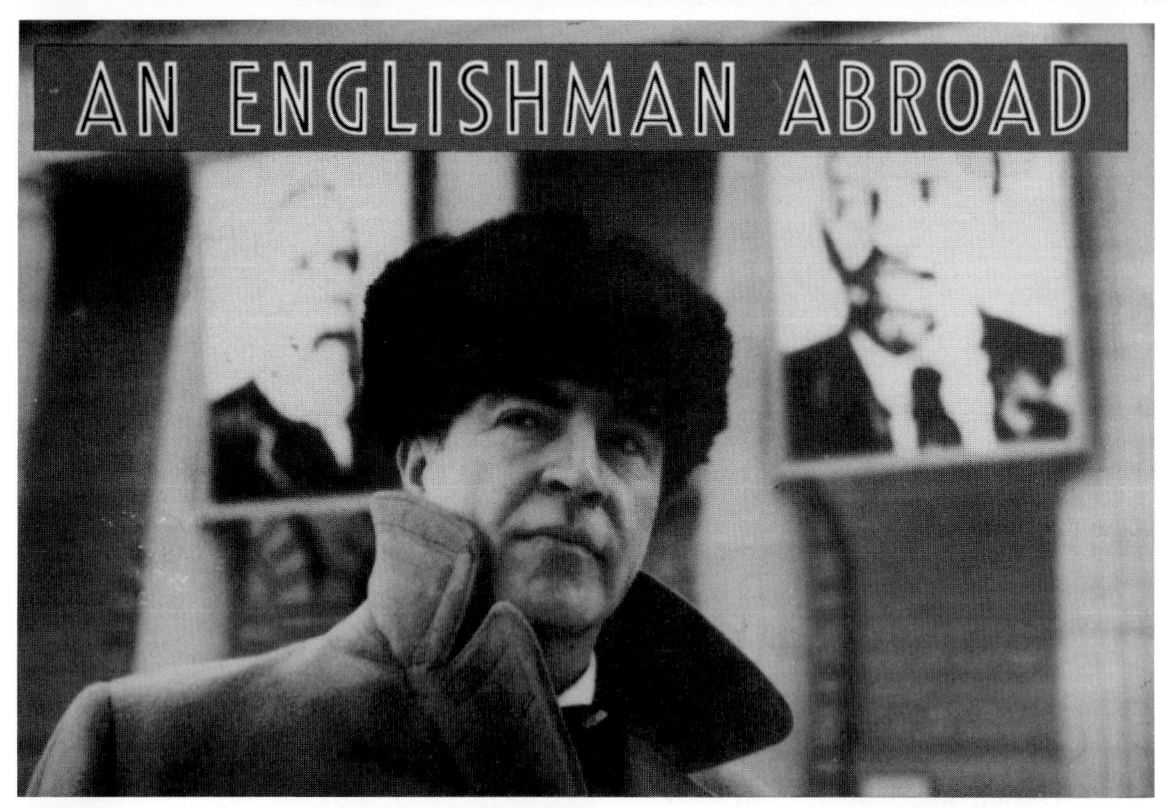

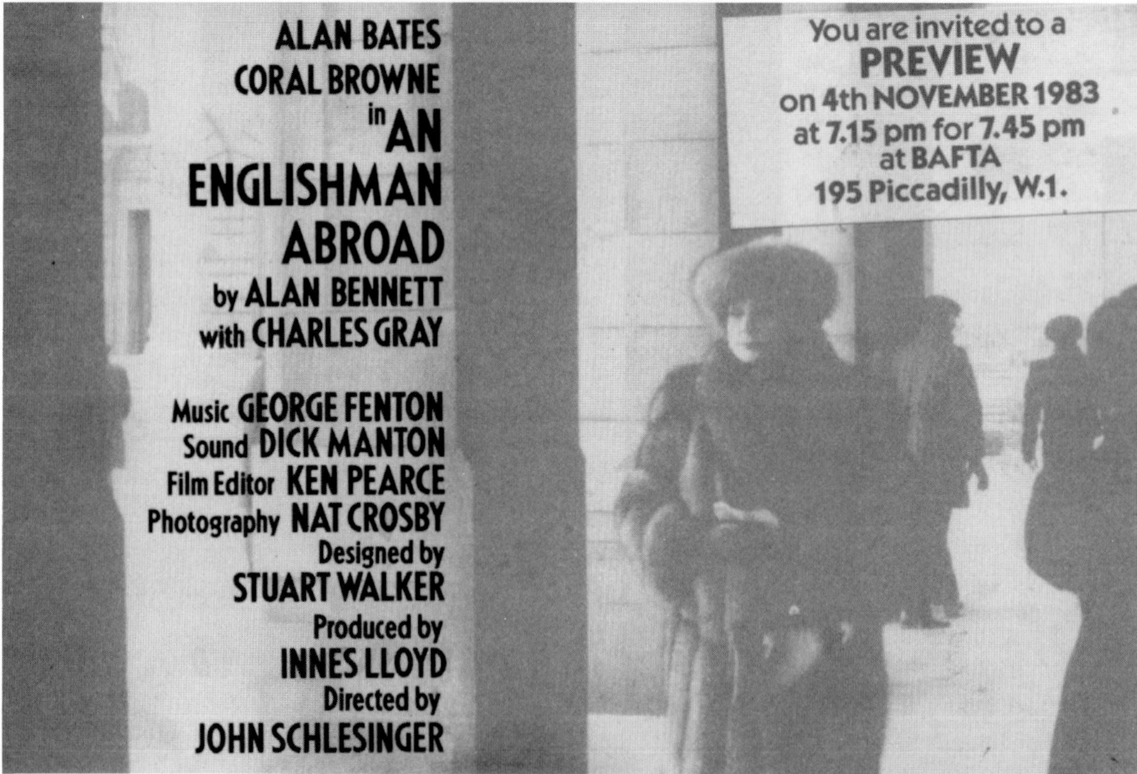

An invitation to the preview of *An Englishman Abroad*

'A Doddle'

When John Dunne of personnel all those years ago, had asked me at my interview what job I would like to do, my reply, misguided though it was at that early stage in my career, was sincere. Directing was what I wanted to do. Over the years I have had bit of practice at this. Producers had often chosen me to work with inexperienced directors. They knew that I would not sit there while they were floundering and most of them were grateful to have some discreet guidance. Someone once said that directing a large drama unit was like playing with the world's biggest model railway. Get the signals wrong and you could be heading for disaster

I was discussing this with Innes Lloyd, the producer I had worked for most in the Drama Department. 'Would you *really* like to direct a film?' he asked. I nodded. 'Well in that case I'll have to find you something.'

'Do you really mean that you would let me direct?' I was incredulous.

'Leave it with me,' said the ex Naval Officer. For the rest of the day I walked around in a daze.

A week or two later there was a script in my pigeonhole at Ealing, with a note from Innes. 'Tell me what you think of this.'

The script was for a 30-minute film drama, based on a true story. In 1939 just before the outbreak of World War Two, a British submarine, the *Thetis*, was on her trials off the coast near Portsmouth. While submerged, she was involved in a collision, and water began entering the hull. She was resting on the bottom with only a few feet of water above her. A flotilla of rescue boats was soon in attendance. Divers were hurriedly assembled from their stations in Scotland but in spite of the rescue attempts and the attempts by the submarine crew to escape, all of the men in the *Thetis* drowned. Later a tribunal heard of the series of mistakes that had resulted in this tragedy and designs and procedures in submarines were changed as a result.

This was a fascinating project for my first film but it was by no means straightforward. For one thing this was a true story and no doubt there were living relatives of the doomed men. The casting would be critical. Also, it would be difficult to film in a real submarine because of the limited space.

In fact there was a submarine of the same class as *Thetis* on dry land at Portsmouth, and I went down to have a look at her. Some filming could be done there but it wasn't an option for the whole film.

Innes had come up with another idea. A German Production Company had built an accurate full-sized reproduction of a U-boat for the remarkable film *Das Boot*, which could be split in two lengthways, giving room for fluid camera shots. This was now in a studio in Hamburg and Innes's plan was to hire the set, which would be reassembled in the studios at Ealing. U-boats and British submarines of this period were very similar and this should not present a design problem. For the next few weeks I spent every spare moment making storyboards, and thinking about the film.

Then Innes asked to see me. He told me that for various reasons he had decided not to go ahead with this project, mainly because it would be too expensive for a short film. I thought that my big chance had come and gone. I put a brave face on it and tried not to look too disappointed. Innes spread his hands on the desk. 'Sorry,' he said, 'I know how disappointed you must be.' After a pause he brightened. 'However,' he said in his country gentleman's voice, I have a script here from Roger Milner, which I would like to do. He handed me a considerably thicker script than the *Thetis* project. 'It's a Play for Today about the aviator Amy Johnson,' he said. 'It runs for about 95 minutes. It's a doddle,' he added, no doubt seeing the fear in my eyes, 'a few flying sequences, air to air, that sort of thing. You'll love it.'

The next few months were probably the most exciting in my life. I of course, loved my work as a DP (Director of Photography) in spite of it being a pretty exhausting life-style. Dramas are usually shot over 6-day weeks, 14 to 16 hours a day. I often did them almost back-to-back and the pressures get to you. Dragging oneself out of bed at some unearthly hour of the morning and battling round the M25 can be a little wearying. When I lived in the north-east of London all the locations were inevitably in the south-west. As soon as I moved to the south-west, all locations moved to the north-east. Usually by about mid-way into a drama. I would feel almost permanently tired. As a Director, preparing to film *Amy,* things were completely different. I felt alive and had inexhaustible energy. Every moment was a new challenge. I was permanently two feet off the ground.

My cameraman was to be Remi Adesfarin. I knew I would get along with him and liked his work. Another old mate, Dick Manton, was to do the sound. Dick was known for doing excellent work without any fuss.

Innes and I then concentrated on casting. It would have been foolhardy of me not to rely heavily on his experience for this. But I did have a strong idea for the part of Amy Johnson. I had seen an actress in *The Imitation Game* and thought that she would be ideal. Innes wasn't sure at first, but he came round eventually. Harriet Walter was sent the script and she said she would like to do it.

We spent two weeks in Innes's office seeing actors. I explained to them that because it was my first directorial job I would like them to read a scene for me, although I knew that some big-name actors do not like doing this. However all were happy to comply, apart from one actor who was up for the part of Jim Mollison. He flatly refused, saying he did not do readings. I respected this but decided that if we couldn't agree at this early stage it did not bode well for the six weeks of filming, so he didn't get the part. In the end Clive Francis played Jim Mollison and I thought he gave a charismatic performance and brought a lot to the character of Amy's competitive and wayward husband.

The designer was John O'Hara, chosen by Innes for his interest in aviation. He was a member of the BBC flying club and was a qualified pilot. This proved to be

Harriet Walter as Amy Johnson and Clive Francis as her husband, Jim Mollison

very useful. I was living in Surrey at the time, ten minutes drive from Fairoakes Airfield in Chobham. When we were doing 'recces' looking for an airfield with a 1930s look, John would pick me up at Fairoakes in his Cessna, and we would do our location-spotting from the air. Although I was a non-pilot, on level flight, he would let me take over the controls.

We finally settled for Sywell Airfield in Northamptonshire as the main location. It had several period hangars and part of it could be transformed into Darwin, for the scenes of Amy's triumphant arrival in Australia. It was also a pretty quiet location without jet aircraft, so there shouldn't be too many hold-ups while shooting dialogue. The club-room of the London Aeroplane Flying Club was to be built in one of the hangars, as was a mock-up of an aircraft cockpit to cut into newsreel shots of the real Amy Johnson and Jim Mollison during their record breaking attempts. The flying of some of the vintage aircraft was to be in the hands of Henry Labouchère and Cliff Lovell and other pilots of the De Havilland Moth Club. A flyable replica of Amy's Gypsy Moth, *Jason*, complete with the correct markings was to be used for air-to-air shots of Amy in the open cockpit. Since actresses can't necessarily be expected to fly, one of the pilots would double for Harriet wearing her costume and a wig. However Harriet was game enough to sit in the open cockpit of a Gypsy Moth, with a camera strapped to its wing, while the pilot looped the loop several times.

One thing I learned about being a director is that you spend a large part of the day answering questions. The wardrobe department fires them at you as do make-up, design, production and so on. I was given a wonderful lady called Irene East as my production assistant, and what she didn't know about the production side of things, wasn't worth knowing. Peter Kondal was my first assistant director, and he kept me under control when some of my ideas became too wild.

I was given an office at the Television Centre and preparations, casting and rehearsals proceeded. The shooting date seemed a reassuringly long time ahead until one Friday, when my butterflies staged a mass rally as I realised that we were to begin filming the following Monday. As a cameraman I was always nervous on the first day of a new drama, but this time I was so tense it felt as if every muscle was encased in concrete. I had no worries about the mechanics of filming, the constructing of sequences and the telling of a story. But working with actors was a new experience, and I just hoped I could coax from them the best performance of which they were capable. It was heady alchemy; I hoped to discover the formulae. Matters were not made any easier by the weather on that first shooting day. There was a howling gale, which made it impossible to fly in the Gypsy Moths.

Harriet and the rest of the actors were very responsive and as my confidence grew, I think theirs did in me. I felt that sometimes there was a tendency for me to over-direct and that it was important not to give the actors too much information. When I had watched Stephen Frears directing I noticed that he seemed not to give the actors any notes at all and I was aware that perhaps I was giving them too many, a situation I hope I corrected as shooting proceeded.

In retrospect, Roger's script was quite gently written, and perhaps I should have got some of the characters to be more hard-edged to compensate. Anyway shooting went ahead quite smoothly, I began really enjoying it, and I think everyone else did too. There were flying sequences, plane crashes and domestic upheavals. We ended filming with a week at the London Ritz Hotel where we shot scenes of Amy arriving back early from a function and finding Jim Mollison in bed with two women, leading to the final break up of their marriage. During the filming at the Ritz there was a major power-cut in Piccadilly and filming was held up. I decided to fill in the time by having breakfast in the grand restaurant. 'Breakfast at the Ritz!' I thought. 'I have arrived.' Then the power came on again and it was time to depart.

Then began perhaps the most enjoyable part, the editing. The heat is off, you have the material and it's just you and the film editor, in this case Ken Pearce. I think that this is perhaps the most creative part of the whole process of film-making. It's where the film comes to life, and all sorts of things can be tried that perhaps weren't there originally, like Amy's thoughts when she is in hospital recovering from a nervous breakdown. We used the voices of actors from previous scenes. I know that this is a cliché but it's a useful one, although in retrospect I think I would have handled some of the scenes differently.

The take-offs and landings of Amy Johnson and Jim Mollison's record-breaking attempts had been well covered by the press and newsreels of the day so we had a lot of documentary material to use within our film. By using only long shots of the real Amy and Jim in the newsreels, we were able to get away with cutting to close-ups of Harriet and Clive. Then came the dubbing sessions.

Above: Amy Johnson (Harriet Walter) working as an aeroplane mechanic, hoping someone would sponsor her flight to Australia

Right: My Director's kit

Dudley Simpson had written some original music and I used John Ireland's piano concerto for some of Amy's early flying sequences. I also used a Jack Buchanan number during a newspaper headlines montage. I got the idea from *An Englishman Abroad* where I thought the Buchanan song, 'Who stole my Heart Away?', was used so effectively by John Schlesinger. The words of the song I used, 'Leave a little bit for me' seemed uncannily appropriate to the rivalry between the two aviators. Then there was the song written specially for Amy Johnson after her historic solo flight to Australia, 'Wonderful Amy'. I had always wanted to direct a musical. This I guess was as close as I was going to get.

Amy was transmitted on the 2nd January 1984 at 9.10 p.m. and I was surprised and encouraged by the many favourable press reviews it received. When it was all over and the dust had settled I wondered if I would be given another film to direct. 'Sure,' said Innes, 'but first spend a year directing Coronation Street. There are a lot of out-of-work directors around.' I didn't think I would be happy directing Coronation Street, even supposing that they would have me, so I went back to my day job.

Silas Marner

March 14th 1984. Started preparations for *Silas Marner.* The cast includes Ben Kingsley and Jenny Agutter, and is directed by Giles Foster. From the lighting point of view this is a 'firelight movie.' A large part of the action takes place in a small cottage in the Cotswolds and is lit mainly by the flickering fire in the grate. Over the years various techniques have been used to simulate firelight. (The real thing doesn't look convincing. I know, I've tried!) One of the early methods was to hang rags from a stick and wave it in front of the lights. This looked as awful as it sounds. Then as we entered the electronic age all sorts of equipment was invented to simulate the effect. If you sit in a room lit by firelight, the light does not continually change and flicker and I think that it is distracting and unconvincing to light in this way. I used low soft reflected light sources in *Silas Marner* that only occasionally changed density so that the audience is concentrating on the drama and not being distracted by 'clever' lighting effects. Incidentally when Jenny Agutter first arrived on the set, I noticed that she studied her face in a mirror to check my lighting. She didn't make a comment so presumably she was satisfied

As I write, we are in a movie era where 'special effects' are king. A series of formulaic Hollywood blockbusters are being made in which the poor actors have to grimace and posture in front of a blank blue backcloth, where eventually the objects of their terror will be computed in. Are we still surprised and delighted by multitudes of computerised extras, spectacular storms, avalanches, planetary collisions and other titanic disasters? Do they not work against one of the most powerful of the cinema's qualities, leaving something for the audience's imagination? Of course special effects have been with us ever since the moving picture was invented. But they now seem to have become the sole reason for making the film. However believable and realistic, they are no substitute for a good script. Perhaps it's time for films to get back to the art of telling a good yarn simply and movingly. It seems to me that *Saving Private Ryan, Shakespeare in Love* and *American Beauty* fit these criteria perfectly. Perhaps there's hope after all.

J. B. Priestley

As a child I read several J. B. Priestley novels. I particularly liked one about a seedy group of entertainers touring the country during the war, *The Good Companions* I think it was called. When I was to photograph a piece with him at his home I looked forward to meeting him. A few days beforehand I found a copy of his book *Festival at Farbridge*, a novel that takes place during the Festival of Britain in 1951, and took it along with me for him to sign. We did the interview and afterwards I produced his book, which he signed for me, saying as he puffed at a large cigar, 'A very under-rated book.'

Actress Googie Withers told me she was once invited to dinner with the Priestleys. 'We're going to start off with caviar,' proudly announced J B. 'Do you know this jar cost me an 'undred pounds? Have some, Miss Withers.'

'No thank you,' she replied sweetly, 'I never eat it.' Actually she quite liked it but couldn't bring herself to deprive him of such an expensive delicacy.

With Prince Charles and the crew of Jackanory

A Royal Tale

On the 1st September 1984 we headed for Balmoral to film H.R.H. the Prince of Wales. He was to narrate a story that he had written entitled *The Old Man of Loch Nagar.* We were to film it for the children's programme, Jackanory.

It was a cold and rainy day as we set up the camera about a mile from the castle, looking towards the mountain featured in the Prince's story. Two blonde young girls had arrived from Teleprompt, a company that supplies a device that enables a person appearing on television to read a script whilst apparently looking straight into the camera. The words are scrolled up and reflected in a glass plate placed in front of the camera lens. This is common practice for newsreaders, weather-forecasters and many other performers.

My assistant John Rhodes and I wore our Barbours against the chill but I was a little concerned by the flimsy nature of the Teleprompt girls' clothing. They were wearing very short mini skirts and thin tops and were looking quite blue with the cold. They were offered some extra clothing but refused, being determined to look their glamorous best for the Prince. He arrived resplendent in a kilt and sweater, we were introduced, and he sat on a rock in front of the camera. Unfortunately there was a problem. The driving rain kept hitting the Teleprompt glass in front of the lens. This would have shown up in the picture and my assistant constantly had to wipe the glass. Prince Charles understood the problem and every time we were forced to stop he would say, 'More rain on your windscreen?' If we had panned the camera in another direction this would have solved the problem, but we couldn't do this as we had to look towards the specific mountain in the story. After several attempts we finally got the Prince's story, in close-up and mid-shot. The poor Teleprompt girls by this time were soaked and their carefully arranged hair was now hanging down in rats' tails. Most of their locations were in warm studios and they had underestimated the wild Scottish climate.

Insurance Man

I have worked on three films written by Alan Bennett. *Intensive Care, An Englishman Abroad* and, in July 1985, *The Insurance Man.*

This film is set in Prague so that, of course, is the last place one would think of filming it. In fact for Prague read Bradford and Liverpool. Much of the action takes place in the Workers' Accident Insurance Institute, a nightmarish building where the maimed and disfigured attend day after dreary day in the hope of receiving compensation for injuries incurred at their workplace.

Doctor Kafka works there as a senior executive, eccentric but kind and fair amid a sea of self-important and arrogant officials, clerks and secretaries.

To this extraordinary place a young man Franz arrives. He has contracted a mysterious skin disease, which he thinks must have been caused by his job in a dyeworks. Less intimidated by the bureaucracy than most of the claimants he tries to find someone to listen to his plight. His skin condition has resulted in the loss of both his job and his fiancée, and he desperately wants someone to give a name to the disease that has ruined his life. He finally gets to meet Kafka who is sympathetic and although unable to authorise compensation for Franz, offers him a job in a factory that Kafka's brother-in-law has started. Inexplicably the young man's skin disease disappears as quickly as it arrived, and now he has a new girl friend. His troubles seem to be over and he gratefully accepts Kafka's offered job - in a factory making asbestos.

Innes Lloyd produced and Richard Eyre was the director. Daniel Day Lewis played Kafka and Robert Hines was Franz. I sought a key sentence from Richard to influence my approach. 'Is it like a nightmare?'

'More Alice in Wonderland,' Richard said.

Richard and I watched a scene from Fritz Lang's film *M* depicting a group of heavily back-lit cigar-puffing detectives in a smoke filled room, and that is the image we tried to achieve in one of the scenes. It seems to me that however much one has pre-conceived ideas of how a film will look, as shooting progresses the film seems to develop a life of its own and somehow dictates its own style, visually anyway. Richard wanted me to shoot the film in black and white but I suggested that the viewers would think that they were watching an old film. I persuaded him to let me shoot in very muted colours, almost black and white but not quite. The sets and costumes were made in shades of grey and brown, and the make-up was pale. The film laboratories too were involved in the special processing of the negative.

There is a long corridor in the set of the Workers' Accident Insurance Institute with glassed offices on one side. A secretary moves along visiting each office in turn to collect for one of the staff, who has 'moved upstairs.' (Not died, promoted.) As she visits each office we are introduced to some of the officials as they interview damaged claimants. We finish in the office of Doctor Kafka. Meanwhile the Head of Department strolls along importantly with one of his minions. We decided to do this scene in one continuous seven-minute take. It's always interesting to do this, in spite of the complications. The actors like it because it gives them a chance to give a sustained performance. Every one else on the unit gets involved and it's a good feeling when the take goes well. We placed the camera on a dolly, which moved down the corridor following the secretary into each office until we reach Kafka who emerges from his office and takes us into the Head of Department's scene. One of the problems was that when we were looking into the glass-windowed offices I could see a complete reflection of the camera, crew and director. The Wardrobe department provided some black material to cover us. They found some spare black costumes, which were standing by to clothe the extras. As usual everything was being taken very seriously, but I couldn't help smiling at my grips, Steve Phillips, who was pushing the dolly and looking very macho in an old crone's dress. Director Richard Eyre as befitted his position was dressed in a neat little black ballroom number with a hood. My assistant and I managed to avoid being in drag by having the camera and us covered with a black curtain. The shot worked well. You can see the reflection of the secretary in the glass but no sign of the camera or crew. We did five takes and apart from getting an interesting shot we got seven lovely minutes of script in about an hour. It may not sound much but in filming terms it is.

THE INSURANCE MAN

BY

ALAN BENNETT

Because of the subject matter, I was able to make the lighting and composition quite surreal in a way I rarely can. Fingers of light hit stone stairways and moving shadows are projected from the ancient lift over the unfortunate claimants.

The late Freddie Young, legendary DOP whose work includes *Lawrence of Arabia* and *Dr Zhivago*, was one of the judges of the BAFTA cinematography award in the year of transmission and I felt very privileged to be given it.

Slip Up

November 2nd 85. Shooting *Slip Up*. It's a comedy about the exiled Great Train robber Ronnie Biggs, and his confrontation with a somewhat inept English policeman who has arrived to arrest him, unaware that Brazil had no extradition agreement with the UK. Meanwhile members of the British press are hurtling round in their cars like Keystone Cops, trying to find Biggs and his wife.

The action is set in Rio but we shot it in Lisbon and Alicante, which made a nice change from filming in Bradford. It was directed by James Cellan Jones.

Commercial for the BBC

The BBC decided to make a commercial promoting itself, and in December 1985 I was given the job of photographing it. I think I am right in saying that this was the first time this had been done at the BBC although many have been made since. Alan Parker was hired in to direct. I pre-lit a large pub set which was constructed on one of the stages at Ealing. John Cleese would be seen in close-up talking to the barman and asking, 'What has the BBC ever done for us?' The crowded pub would be full of BBC personalities and performers who would reply to this question in various ways. The idea was based on a sketch in the film *Life of Brian* where John Cleese asks, 'What have the Romans ever done for us?'

Filming took place over two days and the various participants came in to do their close-ups at different time of the day, and then departed. It was all rather like a doctor's waiting room. When everyone's close-ups were cut together it would look as if they were all there at the same time. The cast included Alan Whicker, David Attenborough, Robin Day, Terry Wogan, Melvyn Bragg, Michael Barratt, Jimmy Young, the Tomorrow's World team, various actors, the list went on an on. Alan Parker directed with twinkly good humour until Patrick Moore arrived. He swept in breathlessly saying, 'I can give you ten minutes – I've got a comet to watch.' Alan Parker's jaw dropped. He had never been spoken to by a performer in this way before. He caught my eye and laughed. He realised that this was a BBC species not found in other jungles. Incongruously Patrick is discovered playing a pin-ball machine before turning to deliver his line. We shot his contribution in six minutes and he made a hasty departure to watch his comet.

The next morning Alan Parker and I watched the previous day's rushes. In order to save (public) money the film rushes were printed on short ends of film by the labs at one printer light and were simply used by the film editor as a cutting copy. When edited this was returned to the lab for a high quality 'showprint' to be made from the negative. At the BBC this practice had been going on for years and we were all used to seeing substandard prints of our work at rushes. We relied on the negative reports from the lab as an indication that all was well. Alan Parker did not know of this practice. His shooting was normally done on 35 mm film and not, as in this case 16 mm. He was used to seeing finely graded prints of his rushes and found the quality of the pictures he was watching unacceptable. I tried to explain the BBC method but he was not convinced. There was only one thing for it. I organised a despatch rider to pick up a properly graded print from the labs, which arrived in two hours. When Alan saw this he said, 'That's better. They're rich and juicy.'

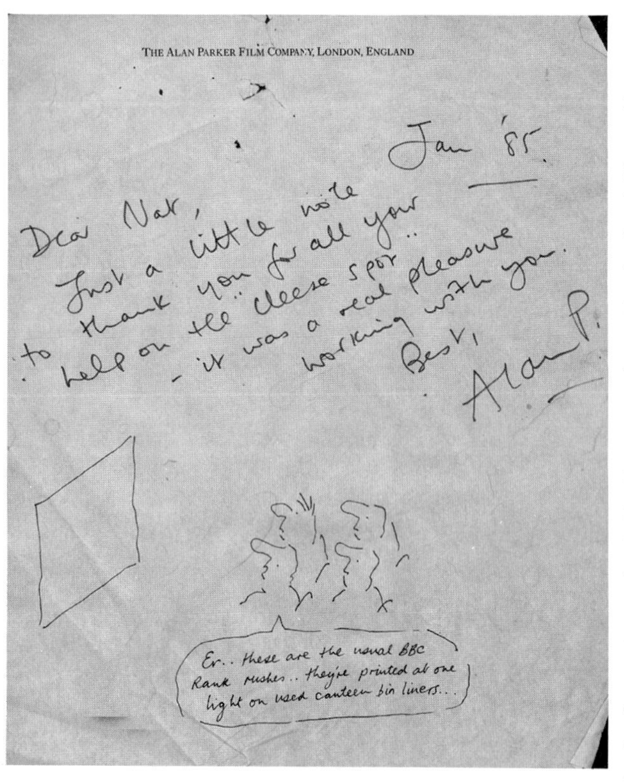

THE ALAN PARKER FILM COMPANY, LONDON, ENGLAND

Jan '85

Dear Nat,

Just a little note to thank you for all your help on the Cheese spot..

– it was a real pleasure working with you.

Best,

Alan P.

A week or so later he sent me a thank you letter with a cartoon that he had drawn of me trying to explain to him that the BBC rushes were printed on old bin liners.

Northanger Abbey

It's highly probable that most people would assume that a dramatised version of a Jane Austen novel would be a model of civilised gentility. When the version of *Northanger Abbey* we shot in 1985 appeared on BBC TV, there were one or two raised eyebrows.

Here's what one viewer thought: Philip Taron of Everson, Washington State, USA.

'I just checked out [the video of] *Northanger Abbey* from the local library, and wasn't expecting much. Imagine my surprise at this gothic treat! Northanger Abbey is one of the most eerie places that you have ever seen, with empty passageways and ornate rooms full of hidden secrets. The glory of the movie is that it never reveals all: your imagination runs free, running with the imagination

of the main character Katherine M. She is a girl of wild imaginations a reader of gothic fantasy that she brings into her (our) real world.

If I were to use one word to describe this excellent movie it would be surrealistic. Dreams are woven throughout the movie, enhancing the mood. Sometimes, it is hard to tell what is real and what is not; this is intentional, I believe.

Atmosphere reigns supreme. The music is not what you'd expect of a movie by Jane Austen: it is eerie, flute and drum-based high and haunting with an undercurrent of fear. If a soft, pleasant tune were playing in Northanger Abbey, it would be positively inviting. Now it is foreboding, a grim and stark-walled palace of a madman. (But the characters! You shall have to see them for yourself!)'

Original music was by Ilona Sekaz, film editor Robin Sales, production design Cecilia Brereton, costume design Nicholas Rocker, make-up designer Joan Stribling. The cast included Katharine Schlesinger, Peter Firth, Robert Hardy, Googie Withers, Geoffrey Chater, Cassie Stuart, Jonathan Coy.

Maggie Wadey did the dramatisation, Giles Foster directed and Louis Marks produced.

East of Ipswich

Michael Palin had written a comedy set in delightful and quirky Southwold and Walberswick in Suffolk.

East of Ipswich. is the story of a fifteen-year-old boy who reluctantly goes on holiday with his parents to Suffolk. They stay at a rather gruesome guest house run by an iron-willed lady who will stand no nonsense from her guests. After breakfast comes the inevitable daily ritual of the trip to the beach with his parents. Then he makes friends with a slightly older boy and is introduced to the mysteries of girls and dating.

After a series of adventures our boy finally loses his virginity to a surly Dutch girl and goes home happier and wiser.

Michael Palin, although not appearing in the film, was on location with the unit. The director was Tristram Powell. Tristram usually worked as a documentary producer and this was his first drama. It was a highly enjoyable production to work on and has become something of a cult film.

EAST
OF
IPSWICH
by
Michael Palin

THE
NATURE
OF THE
BEAST

Poppyland

I have shot many films in Norfolk and it is one of my favourite places. The huge skies and silvery light make it a sought-after location for painters, photographers and film-makers. Its villages and hamlets create a feeling of remoteness far from the noise and confusion of life in a city. (Apart, that is, from the alarmingly low-flying military aircraft that sometimes rip through the sky).

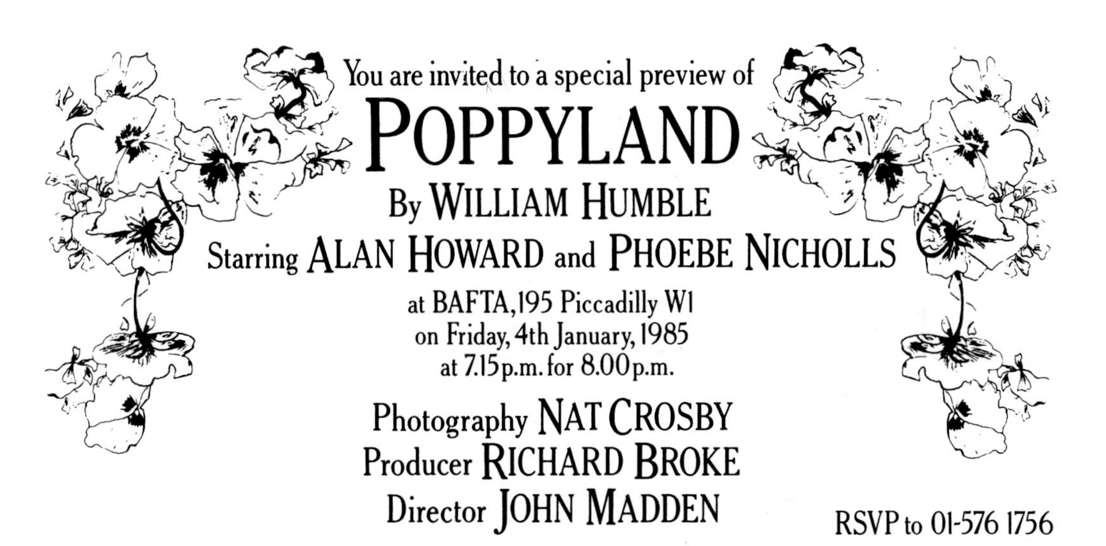

I travelled there again in 1986 to work on the film drama *Poppyland.* It is based on a true story, which took place in the 1880s. Theatre critic and travel writer Clement Scott (Alan Howard) travels to Norfolk to write a piece about Cromer which he finds 'too esplanady' for his taste. He is bewitched by the little unspoiled village of Overstrand and the innocent delights of the little house he stays in, attended to by Louie, the miller's daughter (Phoebe Nicholls), who looks after the very few guests to find this idyllic spot. But inevitably as Scott writes about the place, it becomes a major tourist attraction and he fears that both Poppyland and Louie will lose their untouched innocence. 'This will soon become Bungalow land,' remarks Scott at one point. There is a sad ending to the undeclared love shared over many years by the married Scott and the shy Louie.

John Madden, who had just come from the theatre and has gone on to do some notable work, directed the film.

The interiors of Louie and her father's house were shot in a lovely old flint cottage that was awaiting sale. People must have been shorter in those days for the doorways to the various room, were very low. In spite of signs put up by props to 'mind your head' there was the constant sound of thumps followed by muffled curses and people staggering around holding their heads. Sometimes it felt as if we were in the middle of a Monty Python sketch. I'm afraid I too got knocked for six on a few occasions, much to the delight of my assistant John Rhodes.

The weather only let us down on one occasion. The rest of the country was sweltering in hot sunshine, while we had a thick coastal fog for several days. But then the sun returned.

The film was well received and was described by Phillip Purser as 'a curious, haunting, unclassifiable film'.

Goodbye Beeb

1987 was my last year with the BBC film department. After working there happily for thirty-one years, I had decided to go freelance and attempt to get work on a bigger screen. For the last few years I had been shooting three or four dramas a year and in between lots of little bits and pieces, interviews for talks programmes and so on. By going freelance I could, if not choose what I wanted to do, at least choose what I did not want to do. I was fifty-five and reasoned that if I didn't take the plunge now I never would. The BBC had been very good to me. From being a 'trainee clapper-loader', I had become a cameraman in only four years and had experienced a life filled with travel, adventure and drama. But I felt it was time to see if I could sell my wares in a different market place.

There was another reason. At sixty the BBC threw a retirement party for its staff members with speeches, presentations and all the rest. Being a rather shy person I would have found that excruciatingly embarrassing. Anyway I hate goodbyes.

I found an agent who would take me on (CCA Management) and an accountant to do the paperwork I so loathed. I already had a film to go to. It was a Film Four production, *Nature of the Beast.*

These are my diary entries for the year leading up to my leaving.

7th January	Farming
9th January	Discuss filming Jim'll Fix it
10th January	Shoot for Jim'll Fix it
12th January	Andrew Dillon becomes my assistant
13th January	Standby
14th January	Recce *Time,* a space musical at the Dominion Theatre for Jim'll Fix it'.
15 January	Jim'll Fix It. A viewer wants to appear with Cliff Richards on stage in *Time*. Film in afternoon during a specially staged segment with Cliff and the fixitee. Incredible effects. Large areas of the stage move up and down on hydraulic ramps while huge set pieces fly overhead and forklift trucks roam around with space pods attached to crane arms. The stage manager warns, 'Don't get in the wrong place or you'll

	become a hamburger'. I have fun shooting down on Cliff from one of the pods while being trundled around the stage.
19th January	Prepare to give lecture to trainee designers.
20th January	Give lecture.
21st January	Watch Dog
23rd January	Grading the transmission print of *East of Ipswich* at labs
26th January	Standby. Dreaded paperwork.
27th January	Breakfast *Time* - St Stephen's entrance, House of Commons
28th January	A Question of Sport
29th January	Standby. More paperwork.
3rd February	On the Road - Deer Farming
9th February	Standby. Complete paperwork.
10th February	Tomorrow's World - Wheelchair design
12th February	Watch Dog
15th February	BAFTA-nominees lunch
16th February	Crime Watch – Salisbury
17th February	Crime Watch
18th February	Crime Watch
23rd February	Recce Chesterfield Jim'll Fix it
24th February	Recce Chesterfield Jim'll Fix it.
25th February	Standby
26th February	Shoot Jim'll Fix it, Potholing.
27th February	Standby
28th February	Jim'll Fix it
1st March	Jim'll Fix it
2nd March	Jim'll Fix it
3rd March	Jim'll Fix it
4th March	Standby
5th March	Watch
6th March	Interviewed by *Broadcast* magazine
9th March	Standby
10th March	Meeting with Roy Battersby for possible forthcoming production.
11th March	Standby
12th March	Producer, Peter Goodchild's retirement party. He seemed to enjoy it!
13th March	Dinner at the Savoy for BAFTA nominees.
15th March	Travel by coach to Grenada Television, Manchester with fellow BBC nominee, Ken Westbury, for the BAFTA Awards TV programme. He is up for *The Singing Detective* and I'm convinced he'll get it. I am wrong, I get it with

	Insurance Man. Meet Princess Anne for the third time and Shirley Bassey for the first. Party at hotel afterwards
16 March	Return to Ealing from Manchester about mid-day and find that I have missed a one-hour shoot in London earlier this morning. I am in the doghouse. Not, I feel, the most imaginative scheduling by the Allocations office.
17th March	Standby
18th March	Tomorrow's World. Depart for Stockport
19th March	Shoot Tomorrow's World - System designs
20th March	Return base
29th March	Brands Hatch to shoot 35 mm titles for Outside Broadcast series
30th March	Brands Hatch. Gave up smoking
7th April	40 Minutes. *Love at First Sight*. Huntingdon
8th April	Standby
9th April	Standby
10th April	Standby
11th April	Still haven't smoked.
13th March	Meeting, Ealing
14th April	Standby
21st April	Give lecture to trainees at Neptune House
27th April	Meeting
28th April	Standby
29th April	40 Minutes
30th April	Standby
7th May	Camera Test
8th May	Standby
14th May	Open University, Southampton
27th May	Victoria Wood Show. Recce at BBC studios Birmingham.
28th May	Standby
31st May	Victoria Wood. Depart for Birmingham
1st June	Film sketches with Victoria Wood and Julie Walters as Mrs Overall. Hilarious.
2nd June	Victoria Wood
3rd June	Victoria Wood
4th June	Finish Victoria Wood. Last programme for the Beeb. Nice to end with a laugh
5th June	Return Base
10th June	Meeting with Franco Rossi at Greenpoint
19th June	Farewell drinks with colleagues.

Nature of the Beast

In July 1987 I started work on the *Nature of the Beast,* a Film on Four directed by Franco Rossi. It was a strange feeling no longer being covered by the cosy BBC blanket. I had taken for granted the vast organisation ready to spring into action if problems arose. Now, in a lot of ways, I was on my own and more in command of my own destiny. Not a bad thing I suppose. One aspect I thoroughly approved of was that I no longer had daily forms to fill in, nor did I have to worry about claiming hotel bills and expenses. This was all taken care of by the production.

Near the unit hotel was a BMW garage. My car was a 316, which had seen better days. I celebrated my increase in earnings by swapping it for a new 320i. I travelled to and from the location with Franco Rossi and his wife, so my shiny new car was parked in the hotel car park. One evening as we were returning to the hotel, I saw, from a distance and to my horror, a deep scratch across the red bodywork of my new car. As we slowly approached the BMW in Franco's car, with my heart sinking into my boots, I realised that it wasn't a scratch, but clever artwork by the design department. The rest of the unit, who had been hiding, emerged laughing like a drain. I laughed as well, more from relief than anything else.

Nature of the Beast is set in Accrington and the surrounding moors and is about a mysterious and unseen beast roaming the moors and brutally savaging sheep and other creatures. It is also the story of a lone schoolboy Bill, played by Lynton Dearden. The film has been likened to Ken Loach's 1970 film, *Kes*. Freddie Fletcher, who plays Bill's father in *Nature of the Beast,* played the bullying older brother in *Kes.*

The climax of the film is Bill fleeing from home, finding the beast in the lonely, moonlit moors and confronting it. This was quite a challenging sequence to shoot. The beast although not named in the script was to be represented by a black panther. A large section of moorland was securely fenced off to prevent the panther from escaping. A trench had been dug for the camera and boxed in with a slit, almost at ground level, through which we could film.

It was a night shoot and I had a big HMI light on a 'cherry picker' that flooded the area with 'moonlight.' At about midnight the generator providing power for the lights broke down and plunged us into darkness. The electricians worked feverishly to repair it and by 1.30 a.m. we had light again. It was quite an eerie scene. The members of the film unit had been told to remain behind the fence, and my assistant and I, within the fenced area, crawled into our trench. The animal handlers were quite tense, as wild animals can be unpredictable. The panther was released at a distance from the camera and I was able to get good shots on a long lens of the animal heavily backlit by the 'moonlight', its breath smoking in the cold night air. After a while the panther started to explore its surroundings and slowly made its way towards our camera hide. I kept filming, getting good shots of it approaching us. It got closer and closer until its head filled

Franco Rossi directing a chicken for *Nature of the Beast*

the frame. This made a great shot as it moved out of the picture to the left. I took my eye away from the viewfinder to see where it had gone and to my surprise saw a big black paw with claws like six-inch nails a few inches from my left ear. The panther had pushed one of its front legs through the camera slit to explore the contents. I stepped back rather hastily, not wanting to become a giant pussycat's canapé.

The night shoot had been placed at the end of the shooting schedule and just before dawn we had finished. It was a nice feeling to have completed the filming and we all settled down to a hearty breakfast.

Buy me!

Now that I was a freelance I was free to do commercials. They are quite often just two or three-day shoots and they pay well. However there was just one problem. Producers of commercials watch other people's commercials rather than the programmes. This is a wild generalisation of course and I am sure that there are exceptions, but not that many. I was unknown in the commercial world. Flick from CCA, my agency, said that she would drop my name around.

Sure enough, a couple of weeks later, I had a commercial to shoot. It was for a new brand of margarine and we were to shoot it in a hotel in Surrey. I arrived there on the morning of the shoot and met the director. He knew of my background. 'Don't make it look too easy,' he said. 'I know you ex-television guys can work fast. The clients want to feel that they are getting their money's worth.' I nodded. It was true that I loved working fast. I have a low boredom threshold and like to get on with things. I was going to have to calm down a bit. We started preparing and I lit very deliberately, occasionally changing my mind and starting again. The director nodded his approval. Apart from the large unit in the room, there were three people from the film agency and three clients. The latter are treated like gods as they provide the money, or rather the company that they work for does. (Well actually it's the people who buy the product.) It struck me that the agency people and the client people were really more interested in impressing each other than observing the work. They were all young and they spoke in smart, witty and trendy phrases, each trying to be smarter, wittier and trendier than their colleagues. Every so often one of them would saunter over and make a suggestion to the director in a casual sort of way. He was in an awkward position. If he turned down every suggestion that the clients put to him they would lose face in the eyes of their colleagues, and clients must not be upset. On the other hand if he agreed with too many of their ideas they would wonder if he were worth the enormous salary he was being paid. He coped admirably; after all that was what he was being paid for.

After shooting all day in a fairly relaxed way, the atmosphere changed. There was an air of subdued excitement. It was time for the pack shot. The pack shot is the Holy Grail of the commercial world. It is a close up of the product and has to look luscious and sexy. It must shout 'Buy Me, Buy Me.' Quite a lot to ask from a pack of margarine.

'I am lighting the pack shot. I'd like the room cleared. I'll be an hour.' I said authoritatively to the First Assistant Director. I was getting the hang of this commercial thing. We suspended a large silk sheet over the table where the pack of margarine resided. I then proceeded to pump light through the silk, as never before. The temperature in the room began climbing. I placed gold reflectors around the greasy blonde tablet. Little spotlights caressed its every contour making its creamy surface gleam seductively. This was going to be the sexiest block of margarine ever seen. We were ready and the rest of the unit and the agency and clients came back into the room. There were gasps of 'Wow,' and 'yes!' as they took off some of their clothing because of the heat. Of course the margarine on the table started melting but it was only a stand in. The real star was waiting in the fridge until the last possible moment. That moment came and gloved hands reverently placed it on the table. There was an almost religious atmosphere. The clapperboard was spirited in, the camera turned and the moment was caught on celluloid forever – well, after 20 more takes anyway.

A day or so later I saw the product in a supermarket. Curiosity got the better of me and I bought some. It tasted like cartwheel grease.

Actually that was not the first time I had shot a commercial. Many years ago in the black and white days, a director friend had phoned me. He was in trouble. He was booked to do a week of commercials but his cameraman was involved in a Middle Eastern war and was unable to make it. Could I help him out? I took some leave, hired a camera and joined my friend. The first commercial was for Golden Wonder Crisps and was being shot in a children's playground. It was pretty straightforward stuff and to liven things up a bit, I cut a hole in the bottom of a bag of crisps and stuck the wide-angle lens through it and took the shot from a low angle. The kids taking the crisps from the bag made an interesting shot. The next commercial was for a Twix bar. We had been given some shortbread sticks and a tin of toffee and were required to film the molten toffee being poured over the biscuit. It sounds simple but we couldn't get the melted toffee to coat the biscuit in an appetising-looking way. Finally I had an idea. A tin of Castrol motor oil was obtained from a local garage and looked great as it was poured over the biscuit. I think that now there are laws about using unsuitable materials and there are all sorts of experts at hand to make food products look good. It was much more casual in those days and perhaps more fun. Another shot involved me sitting on a porter's trolley and being trundled along through Shepherds Bush market. As it approached lunchtime and we were very near the BBC studios, I was worried that someone might see me. Shooting commercials was not in my contract. The film people I was working with thought that this was very amusing, and a make-up girl plonked a huge moustache on my upper lip; I don't think it fooled anyone.

Madame Sousatzka

One morning in 1977 I had a phone call from John Schlesinger offering me the job of the cinematographer on a film he was directing, *Madame Sousatzka.* The lead was to be played by Shirley MacLaine. It was to be shot partly on locations in west London with a big scene taking place in the Albert Hall. There were also two major interiors being built at Twickenham Studios where a lot of the action would take place.

During my career I had worked with many well-known actors, but I was still very much the star-struck movie fan. One of my favourite films was *Sweet Charity* in which Shirley MacLaine had given a triumphant performance. I could hardly believe that now I was to photograph her. John Schlesinger's production was probably the biggest picture I had ever worked on. It was to be shot on 35 mm and was of course being made for the cinema. To say that I was a little nervous would have been an understatement.

Paul Emmons describes the plot.

'Manek, (Navin Chowdhry) a brilliant 15-year old pianist in modern London, is the son of a poor divorcee from India (Shabana Azmi). His school arranges lessons for him with Mme Sousatzka, (Shirley MacLaine) a formidably competent, dedicated and eccentric spinster. She takes him completely under her wing, teaching him how to live as well as how to play, because everything is connected. The other interesting residents and visitors to her crumbling old apartment house include an ambitious impresario (Leigh Lawson) eager to arrange concert appearances for him She passionately opposes this, because Manek is not ready. But when his mother loses her job, Manek can no longer resist the temptation to start earning money with his talent.'

The script was adapted from a book by Bernice Rubens, and the writing credits include Ruth Prawer Jhabvala and John Schlesinger. The Producer was Robin Dalton.

When I met Shirley MacLaine we talked about *Sweet Charity* and the character she played, a 'taxi dancer' in a sleazy dance hall. Federico Fellini wrote the screenplay and it was directed by Bob Fosse. In the book the dance hall is actually a brothel but it was felt at the time that depicting it as such would alienate audiences. She said she had argued that if her place of work were to be shown as a brothel it would make the ending much stronger. But the producers were adamant that cinema audiences in 1979, particularly in America, weren't ready for such subjects in a musical.

Shirley MacLaine as Madame Sousatzka

After the final shot! The crew and cast of Madame Sousatzka
Twiggy and her husband, Leigh Lawson, in the second row, Shabana Azmi, Shirley MacLaine and John Schlesinger in the third row

We started shooting *Madame Sousatzka* in the apartment house in West London. The cast included Peggy Ashcroft, Twiggy Lawson, Geoffrey Bayldon and Lee Montague.

Lighting Miss MacLaine presented me with something of a problem. She was playing a 50 something spinster, but my instinct with actresses who are not in the first flush of youth, is to light them in such a way as to make them look younger. When we saw the first rushes Shirley said, 'I look too young,' though she didn't protest with much conviction. I had a special light called a 'biscuit tin', so named because that's what it looked like. It had a very diffused lamp inside connected to a dimmer. I used this for Miss MacLaine's close-ups, with the biscuit tin close, slightly below, and dimmed to a soft glow. On one occasion she was watching me set the light and she said, 'Ten years ago I would have killed for one of those'.

While we were on location we would see the previous day's work every evening at the local cinema, which had been hired for our use. It was a big thrill for me to see the 35 mm rushes on a gigantic cinema screen. They looked so beautiful that I had to convince myself that it was I who had shot them.

The London Symphony Orchestra was featured as Manek plays his first and somewhat disastrous big concert.

We spent all night lighting the Royal Albert Hall for another concert sequence. Because of the subject, music naturally played a big part in the story.

As luck would have it, the filming took place during the notorious hurricane of 1987. I was living at the top of a hill in Surrey at the time, and early one morning, having slept through the violent storms in the night, I staggered out of the house to leave for the studio. A scene of devastation greeted me. Several trees were down and a large oak had come down just beyond the garden gate making it impossible for me to get my car out of the drive. The power lines had been severed but the phone was still working. I rang the production office almost hoping that they would say, 'O.K. no problem, go back to bed.' In fact they said, 'Stay put, we will send a car to pick you up at the other side of the tree.'

At the beginning of the shoot, Shirley MacLaine had given me a crystal. 'This will help when the going gets tough,' she had said. I think it did.

When the film had been completed, we learnt that it had been selected for the Royal Film performance and was to be shown at the Empire Leicester Square in the presence of the Queen Mother. After the première we all went to the Savoy for dinner. Normally in this profession, there isn't as much glamour as some people seem to think, but that night it was there in spades.

A Private Life

That year (1988) my assistant Mark and I travelled to Cape Town to shoot a drama based on a true story. The Producer was Francis Gerard. The rest of the crew and the actors lived in South Africa.

The cast and crew for *A Private Life* in South Africa

A Private Life is a love story between a white policeman, Jack, and an Asian girl, Stella. They met when Jack visited a café in which Stella worked. Their meeting took place during *apartheid*, still in force at the time of our filming. It was forbidden for whites and coloureds to have relationships and the fact that the white man was a policeman would have meant imprisonment if they had been discovered. For years they conducted their relationship in secret, had children and educated them at home not daring to send them to school. When their son Paul became a teenager and had a girl friend, he became confused and unable to come to terms with his mixed parentage. One terrible night he threw himself under a train.

We met the original Jack and Stella, now an elderly couple; their feelings for each other unchanged.

Bill Flynn and Jana Cilliers played Jack and Stella. The filming had to be discreet as the script that had been submitted to the authorities was not the one we were shooting. The Cape Town crew were extremely hospitable and we were invited to their homes and taken on excursions on our rest days. They were used to Big American Film Units arriving and shooting 'blockbusters' and they were impressed by the fact that we were making a serious film. *A Private Life* was shown on Channel 4 and at the London Film Festival.

Monster Maker

In 1989 I shot a film called *Monster Maker* with the Jim Henson team. It was a children's story set in the Jim Henson Creature Workshops. A boy with an unhappy home life wants to work in special effects. He breaks in to the studio at night to look at a gigantic dragon-like creature, which has been built for a film. Unattended by its human puppeteers, it comes to life and is instrumental in the capture of the boy's father, who happens to be a burglar. Father and son are reconciled and all is well in the end. My old friend Giles Foster directed this unusual film and it was fun to shoot.

Soul for sale

The commercials were still coming in thick and fast. I got stuck in to them though I had an uneasy feeling that I was selling my soul along with the beer, Sunday newspapers, computers, telephones, margarine, chocolate, sofas and building societies. Still, they paid the mortgage.

Recently I feel the quality of the writing, directing and photography on commercials has been exceptionally good. There are some I would rather watch than the programmes draped on either side of them!

Paper Mask

In October 1989 I started work on a thriller, *Paper Mask.* It is about a young hospital porter who assumes the persona of the doctor who has been killed in a car crash. He applies for and gets a job in a new hospital and his deception goes unnoticed in spite of his mistakes, one of which results in a patient's death.

A nurse falls in love with him and is taken in by his persuasive charm. When a porter friend arrives from his old hospital and threatens to expose his deceit, he takes him for a drive to Cheddar Gorge and throws him off the top. The porter although badly injured survives and is brought back to the hospital to be operated on by the fake doctor.

Paul McGann played the doctor and Amanda Donohue, the nurse. The film was directed by Christopher Morahan, whom I had worked with before on a BBC film, *The Secret State.* Christopher is not the easiest director to work with. On the first day of shooting we were preparing for a scene where the fake doctor is facing an interview board for a job at the new hospital. I had lit the room where six or so actors would be sitting. When the actors were in place, and had had a rehearsal, I could see that one of the lights needed to be adjusted. 'Can you give me two minutes to adjust a light, Chris?' I said.

'I will this time,' he hissed. 'Today I'm being *nice.*' My heart sank. Six weeks of shooting lay ahead, and this was him being nice!

With Chris Morahan filming *The Secret State*

We ploughed on, shooting the hospital scenes in a disused hospital in Balham. It was the usual long day, early start and late finish six days a week, which the film industry sees as acceptable working practice. No one ever protests in the freelance world for fear of not being employed again.

We had reached the last week of filming and were shooting interior and exterior scenes in Bristol. I was sitting at the camera because I was operating as well as lighting. The Director, even more abrasive than usual, was droning on complaining about something or other. I idly thought, as prisoners must think, 'wouldn't it be wonderful to be able to leave this room and just walk around Woolworths'. I looked around me. There were about twelve of the unit in the room, more outside, make-up girls, electricians, the grip, prop boys, the gaffer, the clapper-loader, first assistant, continuity. The ones that were standing were swaying slightly with fatigue. They were desperately trying to look alert, responsive, uncomplaining, as the profession demanded. My assistant Mark was alongside the camera, operating the focus control. I turned to him. Surprising myself I said, 'Do you know, I think I hate this business?'

A poem by W. B. Yeats came into my mind, one that I had learnt as a schoolboy.

I must arise and go now
And go to Innisfree
And a small cabin build there
Of clay and wattles made
Nine bean rows will I have there
And a hive for the honey bee
And live alone in the bee loud glade.

Innes Lloyd

In 1991 Innes Lloyd the BBC producer who had given me my chance to direct, who had always encouraged me, who had produced some of the most memorable films on BBC TV, died of cancer. I was invited to a viewing of his last film, *A Question of Attribution*, directed by John Schlesinger with cinematographer John Hooper. Many old friends and colleagues were there. We all filed up the BAFTA staircase to the viewing theatre. Before the film started a spotlight appeared at the side of the empty stage. It was where Innes had on so many occasions made his introductory speech at a viewing. It was an emotional and silent moment. After the film the audience slowly ambled out of the theatre.

There was dear old John Schlesinger waiting for reactions as we moved past. I thought it a great film and told him so.

I must arise and go now

My bee loud glade is in a tiny village in North Norfolk. I still make films using the latest technology, a marvellous little Sony digital camera. They are films about the village and its occupants. I made one for the millennium celebrations. It featured short pieces to camera from the 100 or so inhabitants of the two adjoining villages, a sort of video Doomsday Book. I am the writer, the director and the cameraman. I edit the films on my Apple Mac computer. We had our première in the packed village hall.

I also write and produce short dramas, and enter them into film festivals.

I didn't have to travel very far to film the last one, a mystery called *The White Dress.* The location was my garden. Bliss.

The End

With Vince in Norfolk